PENNSYLVANIA
MOUNTAIN
LANDMARKS

Pennsylvania Mountain Landmarks

VOLUME 2

Jeffrey R. Frazier

an imprint of Sunbury Press, Inc.
Mechanicsburg, PA USA

an imprint of Sunbury Press, Inc.
Mechanicsburg, PA USA

Copyright © 2023 by Jeffrey R. Frazier.
Cover Copyright © 2023 by Sunbury Press, Inc.

Sunbury Press supports copyright. Copyright fuels creativity, encourages diverse voices, promotes free speech, and creates a vibrant culture. Thank you for buying an authorized edition of this book and for complying with copyright laws. Except for the quotation of short passages for the purpose of criticism and review, no part of this publication may be reproduced, scanned, or distributed in any form without permission. You are supporting writers and allowing Sunbury Press to continue to publish books for every reader. For information contact Sunbury Press, Inc., Subsidiary Rights Dept., PO Box 548, Boiling Springs, PA 17007 USA or legal@sunburypress.com.

For information about special discounts for bulk purchases, please contact Sunbury Press Orders Dept. at (855) 338-8359 or orders@sunburypress.com.

To request one of our authors for speaking engagements or book signings, please contact Sunbury Press Publicity Dept. at publicity@sunburypress.com.

FIRST CATAMOUNT PRESS EDITION: September 2023

Set in Adobe Garamond | Interior design by Crystal Devine | Cover by Lawrence Knorr | Edited by Lawrence Knorr.

Publisher's Cataloging-in-Publication Data
Names: Frazier, Jeffrey R., author.
Title: Pennsylvania mountain landmarks volume 2 / Jeffrey R. Frazier.
Description: First trade paperback edition. | Mechanicsburg, PA : Catamount Press, 2023.
Summary: Pennsylvania hikers know how rugged our mountain trails can be, but also how alluring they are; often causing us to wonder just what's around the next bend in the path. Just like in volume 1, this second volume in the Pennsylvania Mountain Landmarks series provides some clues, and as in the first volume also affords an armchair journey to some of the most unusual and inaccessible landmarks that can be found in the mountains of Pennsylvania.
Identifiers: ISBN : 979-8-88819-135-4 (paperback) | ISBN : 979-8-88819-136-1 (ePub).
Subjects: NATURE / Ecosystems & Habitats / Mountains | HISTORY / United States / State & Local / Middle Atlantic (DC, DE, MD, NJ, NY, PA) | SPORTS & RECREATION / Hiking.

Product of the United States of America
0 1 1 2 3 5 8 13 21 34 55

Continue the Enlightenment!

CONTENTS

Acknowledgments		vii
Introduction		1
1.	The Standing Stone (Huntingdon County)	5
2.	Sentinel Rock (Franklin County)	11
3.	Indian Head Rock (Columbia County)	17
4.	Ole Bull's Castle (Potter County)	23
5.	Blue Hill (Northumberland County)	31
6.	King Wi-Daagh's Grave (Lycoming County)	41
7.	Hoodoo – They Think They're Fooling (Huntingdon County)	50
8.	Towering Above The Rest (Elk/Sullivan Counties)	58
9.	A Heavenly Path (Jefferson County et. al.)	68
10.	Native American Mementoes (Centre County et. al.)	76
11.	The Witness Tree (Centre County)	87
12.	Lochabar (Lycoming County)	96
13.	A Timely Reminder (Union County)	104
14.	Beartown Rocks (Centre and Jefferson Counties)	110
15.	The Rock Garden (Sullivan County)	116
Bibliography		124
About the Author		126

ACKNOWLEDGMENTS

This book and the eight volumes in my Pennsylvania Fireside Tales series would not have been possible without the love and support I received from both of my wives, who predeceased me in tragic ways. My last wife often joked with friends that I would often say to her after supper, "I'm going up to my den and write for about an hour," when, in fact, it would often be more like two hours or more.

Anyone who is a writer will know how that happens. When you start writing, all other thoughts and worries disappear. The words just seem to flow, and thoughts about how to organize those words magically occur. I have never had the proverbial "writer's block"; just starting to write seems to eliminate that nemesis for me, and I think having a loving relationship with my wife at the time was responsible for that. So I dedicate this *Volume 2* of the Pennsylvania Mountain Landmarks series to both of my former wives.

INTRODUCTION

In this second volume of Pennsylvania Mountain Landmarks, the reader will, as in *Volume One*, find more chapters about those unusual and spectacular mountain landmarks that grace the hills of Pennsylvania. And, like those in the first volume, many of these unique spots are not easily found. Likewise, many are even less easily accessed, most requiring navigation along tortuous and steep sylvan pathways to reach them. Nonetheless, to those who enjoy that kind of challenge, the efforts are amply rewarded by the opportunity to gaze upon sights and natural wonders not often seen by many.

At least, that is the way I've felt over the years as I have searched for and made strenuous treks to these very spots. It has often required much patience and determination to find them, usually needing three, and sometimes four, trips to locate them. It has also meant staying in good physical condition, for the mountain trails to get to these out-of-the-way locations, often perched on high mountain tops, would not have been possible otherwise.

But as an author, I wanted to get a sense of place and see first-hand the flora and fauna found there, thus allowing me to write about them with more authority and accuracy. That approach, I felt, would add to the reader's enjoyment, as it would be the next best thing to being there themselves. An "armchair journey" would still be enjoyable since the hassles of the search and the effort to find and get to them are no longer a factor. Nonetheless, for those who must see them for themselves, I have, as in

Volume 1, included GPS coordinates and driving directions in each chapter to facilitate the quest.

But likewise, it is the history and legendary lore that cling to these spots that continued to fascinate me as I sought them out. Hence, as in *Volume 1*, in each chapter, I've included some of these accounts that seemed most interesting to me and would appeal to the reader. So in this volume, look for a Franklin County tale about the Indian sentry whose spirit was cast into the rocks when he failed at his assigned guard duty.

Herein is also a Potter County story about the haunting strains of a violin that some say is nothing more than the wind but which others believe emanate from where there once stood the imposing remains of a large stone castle that dominated a nearby mountaintop. From there, journey to a towering rock monolith in Elk County that once served as a Native American landmark and is haunted by a phantom bobcat!

Although most of the places mentioned are natural landmarks, there is one that, although manmade, is, in my estimation, still one of the most quintessential landmarks in the entire state. And, as before, the charming tales of this place, noted for its genuine "skeleton in the closet," and similar accounts in the other chapters, capture the same mystique of Pennsylvania's earliest times that the tales in *Volume 1* so vividly preserve; accounts of the days of its first settlers and its native sons that are the threads of that colorful patchwork of history and romance that imbue the hills of Pennsylvania with song and legend.

I intended to present this book as a single volume, but much to my delight, my publisher suggested we do it as a three-volume series to make each volume more affordable. That approach also makes it possible to include more photos in each volume since the spots visited deserve to be shown from many angles. Concerning the photos, I've taken most myself. I have also relied upon others and have noted those cases in attributions under the photos. I am grateful that they can be included herein.

My publisher has also expressed interest in taking over my self-published Pennsylvania Fireside Tales series and publishing it under his auspices. I've heartily agreed to that collaboration and look forward to working with him. Readers who enjoy the stories in the Pennsylvania Mountain Landmarks series will do well to consider reading those in my

Pennsylvania Fireside Tales series since they contain many more accounts of the same kind.

I continue to be amazed at the many other interesting natural landmarks I continue to discover in Pennsylvania, and I'd like to explore them all in the future. If I do so, maybe look for a *Pennsylvania Mountain Landmarks Volume 4*! However, at age 77, I have other books I want to write first, and besides, I may be past the point of trying to be Pennsylvania's Indiana Jones of movie fame! Nonetheless, I still hope to instill in my readers an enhanced appreciation for the natural beauty and woodlands of Pennsylvania and, in doing so, inspire them to advocate for the preservation of it.

The cover picture of this volume shows the author standing in front of one of the state's most iconic landmarks. In Elk County on State Game Lands #44, Tomahawk Rock is part of the Indian Rocks formation along the Clarion River. See Chapter 8, "Towering Above the Rest," in this volume for more details about this natural wonder and the haunting image decorating its surface. The same chapter includes details about other towering rock formations similar to Tomahawk Rock which are just as awe-inspiring.

CHAPTER 1

THE STANDING STONE

Anyone who has visited the County Seat of Huntingdon County may recall seeing the remarkable stone obelisk standing at the intersection of Penn and William Smith Streets in downtown Huntingdon. Not a mountaintop sculpture, but an interesting "sculpture," nonetheless, with some interesting history surrounding it, so I've elected to include it with the others mentioned in this book.

The site of the town of Huntingdon was chosen in 1767 by the Rev. Dr. William Smith, who later rose to fame as the first provost of what at that time was called the "College of Philadelphia," later to become the University of Pennsylvania. Along the Juniata River, where Standing Stone Creek flows, Smith's new town was also situated on the spot famous for being an Indian council ground during an earlier day.[1]

It had been named Standing Stone by Indian traders who had traveled through here in prior decades and noticed the large stone obelisk, which the traders learned had been erected by the local Indians. Smith, however, elected to call his town Huntingdon in honor of his English patron, Selina, Countess of Huntingdon, England. But the former appellation, Standing Stone, was still used by older residents of the area for many years afterward.

The Indians' standing stone was no longer there when Smith arrived, and except for a brief mention of it by John Harris, founder of Harrisburg, in his travel log when he passed through here in 1754, we would have no idea of its dimensions. Harris described the stone as being 14 feet tall and

---

1. J. Simpson Africa, *History of Huntingdon and Blair Counties, Pennsylvania*, 434–435.

The Standing Stone in 2018.

six inches square, and on it, he explained, were numerous designs, symbols, and pictographs that were of some significance to the Indians. He did not record or describe what those symbols looked like but surmised the Indians must have placed them there for historical or religious reasons.[2]

He was fortunate to have seen the monolith at all because shortly afterward, the Indians, said to be the Oneidas, a branch of the great Six Nations Indian Confederacy, apparently took it with them when they were forced to leave their Juniata homelands following the signing of an Indian treaty in Albany, New York, that same year. That at least was the assumption since no one knew who else would have wanted it and because it was recalled that

---

2. Pennsylvania Archives (*First Series, II*, 135-136) and Africa (ibid), 46.

the Indians had always venerated it. They did so, said those familiar with the Indians' thoughts, because they believed that if it ever were destroyed or stolen, their tribe would be destroyed by their enemies.[3]

Not too many years later, residents of the community that now occupied the place where the Indians once met in their great councils decided to erect another standing stone that would be an exact duplicate of the original and stand in the same spot. This second monument stood in place as a reminder of the town's heritage for years until "drunken fools," as they were later described, broke it into pieces one night, presumably for no other reason than to destroy something that was appreciated by so many.[4]

A fragment of that second column is still displayed in the main corridor of the Huntingdon County Courthouse, and on the smooth dark-gray face of the stone relic are numerous names and dates scratched upon it by surveyors and town officials of the late eighteenth and early nineteenth centuries.

Then in 1896, a local industrialist proposed erecting another standing stone as part of the town's centennial anniversary celebration preparations. After that, this third stone would commemorate the town's rich history and colorful past, so his proposal was met with enthusiasm. It is this stone that still keeps a silent watch over the town today.[5]

Those who read the history of the Juniata Valley and its Standing Stone will soon come to realize that it is an area steeped in story and legend, and probably the tale that once caused the greatest stir here was that of the mysterious lights that periodically appeared on top of Rocky Ridge near the village of Bridgeport, usually during January.

It was a strange place for lights to appear, being so far away from any settlements and in such an inaccessible spot, and so the matter stood for some time until three gentlemen decided to solve the mystery once and for all one cold December evening in 1889. It took a long hard climb to get there that night, and when the intrepid explorers got near the spot on the mountain where the lights had been seen, they were a bit winded and tired.

---

3. Milton Scott Lytle, *History of Huntingdon County in the State of Pennsylvania*, pages 18 and 26.
4. Sherman Day, *Historical Collections of the State of Pennsylvania*, 370.
5. Found on the web at https://huntingdonboro.com/history/.

Perhaps that's why they were so easily startled when an eerie light suddenly flashed before their eyes.

Much to their astonishment, they saw three lights, looking much like miniature rockets, pop up out of the ground in succession. Each one would then hover for a few minutes before disappearing in the same order they had appeared. Their dim luminescence in the silent darkness of the forest was enough to deter the men from further investigation that night, and they agreed that since the lights must be of some significance, a trip back during the daytime was warranted.

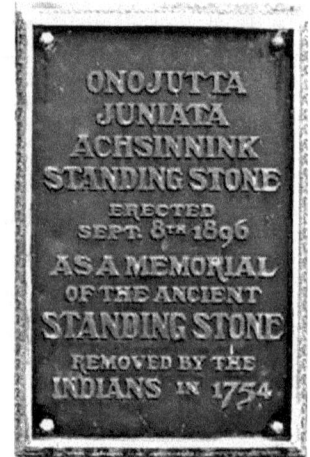

The plaque on the Standing Stone.

Several days later, the same three men, carrying picks and shovels, returned to the same spot and began digging. What happened next was published the following day in a Huntingdon County newspaper article titled "Armstrong's Resting Place."

"After digging into the ground for a depth of six feet, they came upon a pile of loose stones, which covered two large flat stones that formed a lid, upon lifting which they discovered what seemed to be the remains of a human body in a hole about three feet long. The remains were decomposed to a blackened powder, and the bones, when exposed to air, crumbled into dust.

"The explorers made a thorough examination and are of the opinion that someone had been murdered near that place many years ago, and the body had been secreted in this secluded spot, the only thing to mark it being the singular light. What caused the light is as much mystery as ever. Can it be explained upon any scientific, psychological, or mythological theory?

"It is now conceded by many that these were none other than the remains of the notorious Jack Armstrong, an individual who resided near what is known as Jack's Spring, so named after him, on Jack's Mountain, a short distance from Mount Union. He was an Indian trader, and he and two companions were murdered by a Delaware Indian named Musemeelin, in the narrows, about the middle of February 1744.

Fragment of the Second Monument on display in the Huntingdon County Courthouse.

"According to John Harris, the Narrows took their name from Jack Armstrong. He mentions them as Jack Armstrong's Narrows, 'so called from his being there murdered.' Harris' memorandum also pinpoints the site of the massacre of Armstrong and his party. He fixes it at eight miles from Aughwick and ten miles from Standing Stone, which is about the spot where the body was recently discovered."[6]

I've hiked into the Rocky Ridge Natural Area (see the chapter in this book titled "Hoodoo You Think You're Fooling"), and it was not an easy "walk in the park." It would be even more challenging at night, not to mention how intimidating it would be if confronted by the peculiar fireworks

---
6. Albert M. Rung, *Rung's Chronicles of Pennsylvania History*, 230.

that once appeared on this ridge. However, that no longer seems to be something a nocturnal explorer would have to worry about today. According to the January 1889 Huntingdon newspaper account, the lights "have disappeared since the discovery was made!"

There is another standing stone in Pennsylvania that deserves mention because of its historical significance, its unique size and shape, and because it is comparable in some respects to the mighty Pillars of Hercules, once prominent in Greek mythology, that flank the entrance to the Strait of Gibraltar.

According to one early Bradford County historian:

> The name Standing Stone was given to this locality by the Indians on account of a very remarkable stone which stands in the river, near its right-bank. This stone, from the top to the bed of the river, is forty-four feet high; it is sixteen feet wide and about four feet thick. At ordinary low water, the stone is twenty-two or twenty-three feet above the surface of the river. The lower edge of the stone must penetrate the surface of the earth to a considerable depth in order to be able, as it has, to resist the force of the water in freshets and the ice, which, when the river breaks up, suddenly moves with apparently irresistible power. This stone has been a landmark during the history of the county, and the surveys of both the Susquehanna Company and of Pennsylvania refer to it.[7]

LOCATION: The **Standing Stone** monument is located in Huntingdon at the intersection of William Smith Street and Penn Street (Pennsylvania Route 26) and in the median on William Smith Street (DD GPS Coordinates: 40.484796, -78.010281).

---

7. The Reverend David Craft, *1770-1878 History of Bradford County, Pennsylvania with Illustrations and Biographical Sketches of Some of its Prominent Men and Pioneers*, 379.

CHAPTER 2

SENTINEL ROCK

Rothrock's Rock in Franklin County's portion of Michaux State Forest is an iconic spot described in this book's chapter of that name. However, there are many other special spots like this to explore along the trails and mountaintops of the South Mountains in this Pennsylvania outdoor wonderland. Most of these are well pinpointed on topographical and hiking maps of the region, but there is one that is not, and it became the object of some of the most frustrating and fruitless searches your author has ever undertaken while trying to photograph these types of spots over the last fifty years.

It took at least six trips before I found this natural wonder; the quest was interrupted for a year or so after someone mentioned that a mountain lion had been spotted near the peak of the mountain where I had been looking. But by diligently following maps, verbal suggestions, and other leads, my efforts finally paid off one fine summer afternoon near the summit of Rocky Mountain.

This single stone shaft does stand like a silent sentinel along the trail, and it does have a stone burl on one side near the top that could pass for a distorted human face. And all those qualities correspond with the old Indian legend about the rock I was looking for; a rock once called Sentinel Rock. But the facial likeness on the single stone shaft shown in the preceding photograph is not even close to the portrait that could be seen on the original Sentinel Rock; a visage that, in my opinion, was one of the most amazing natural likenesses of a human profile that I have ever seen. And that brings us to why that likeness, according to Native American legend, is there in the first place.

Their account begins in that period of prehistory before white men came to the virgin forests of the South Mountains. At that particular time, there was a tribe of Munsee Indians, or the "Wolf Tribe" as they would have called themselves,[1] living in a remote valley in the shadows of what's now called Rocky Mountain but was once referred to locally as Caledonia Mountain. Given their beautiful surroundings and hard-to-find location, it would have seemed that the Munsees could lead a life of peace and contentment. But that was not the case at all. On the contrary, their nerves were frayed by a need to maintain constant vigilance.

The tribe had to be constantly on guard because some years earlier, they had been in a protracted war with an enemy tribe and, being defeated, fled from them. However, they knew their enemy had vowed to follow them and would not be satisfied until they killed them all. So rather than be subjected to a surprise attack, the Munsees posted an outlook on the mountaintop, day and night, to detect any invaders. The daytime sentinels would have plenty of time to raise the alarm since they could see enemies approaching from miles away. But the nocturnal sentinels would have less time to do so since they would not be able to see invaders until they were almost upon them.

It was therefore decided that certain warning signs should be established. Upon seeing an invading force of the Six Nations coming, the daytime sentinel was to tie a knot of buckskin around an arrow and shoot it into the lodge of his fellow warriors in the valley below. On the other hand, the nighttime sentinel was told to light a bonfire on the mountaintop when he saw a similar invading force coming. These measures were considered sufficient by the tribe, but, as with all such plans, there are always weaknesses, and in this case, the flaw rested with an Indian maiden.

So it happened that late one night, the Indian sentry posted on the mountaintop was surprised by a visit from the daughter of one of the greatest warriors of the tribe. The sleepy sentry told her that this was no place for a woman but craving adventure; she told him that if she stayed with him, the security would be enhanced, that there would be two pairs of eyes to

---

1. Rev. John Heckewelder, *History of the Indian Nations*, 253.

Sentinel Rock. (Photo courtesy of Len Kapp.)

see and two sets of ears to hear. Too tired to argue with her and aroused by her charms, he soon fell asleep in her arms, unaware that a Six Nations war party was approaching.

The silent band of assassins fell upon the unsuspecting couple with their tomahawks, leaving a bloody scene behind as they stealthily made their way down the mountain slope to the sleeping Munsees below. Their subsequent attack was devastating, with a later description claiming that "the arrows fell like hail from an overcast sky" upon their unsuspecting victims.[2]

---

2. "Ancient Legend About Indian Sentry on Caledonia Mountain," article appeared in the *Gettysburg Times* on December 27, 1975, but was reprinted from an article appearing in the *Gettysburg Compiler* on August 21, 1900.

Sentinel Rock as it appeared in 1900. (Photo from an article in the *Gettysburg Compiler.*)

In the end, the slaughter seemed complete, and when the invaders surveyed the scene, they were convinced that they had sent every warrior, woman, and child to a deep sleep from which they would never awake. But somehow, the tribe's witch doctor, or shaman, and the father of the young maiden with the lone sentinel on the mountaintop managed to survive.

Once the enemy warriors had departed, the two surviving Munsees made their way to the mountaintop to find out why they had not been warned as planned, suspecting that their trusted sentinel had failed them.

When they got there, they found the lifeless body of the young maiden, her skull crushed by a vicious blow from a tomahawk. Here also lay the fallen warrior, the life slowly draining from his prostate form.

Close-up of the Indian's face on Sentinel Rock as it looked in 2022. (Photo courtesy of Len Kapp.)

The grief-stricken father and the enraged shaman agreed that, although the wounded warrior was not long for the world, he should be punished for his dereliction of duty. Consequently, the shaman chanted, pausing long enough to tell the dying man that he was casting his spirit into the rocks that towered over this same spot. That from henceforth and for evermore, his spirit was destined to watch the pass. His eyes would be vigilant, and his ears always open, watching and listening for an enemy that would never come.

And for centuries, that curse fastened the spirit of the derelict sentinel to the place where he had failed to carry out his expected duties. For all we know, that still may be the case today, for his visage on the rocks, although once one of nature's most remarkable mountaintop sculptures, is still there today, although less and less evident as years go by.

I was fortunate to find the photo of Sentinel Rock in a newspaper article published in the *Gettysburg Compiler,* dated August 21, 1900.[3] It was in that same article that I found the legend of Sentinel Rock, and from the photo, it was understandable how the Indians might have been inspired to craft their story.

They might have used it to instill responsibility and a strong sense of tribal bonds in their young warriors. That's just a conjecture on my part, and of course, that will never be known, but if the story is true, then the punishment by the Indian shaman must have been powerful; the young warrior's likeness, centuries later, maintains its vigil. Over one hundred and twenty years of weathering and erosion have taken a toll, but its distorted side profile, with forehead, eye, mouth, and chin, still keeps the story alive.

> **LOCATION:** Sentinel Rock is on Caledonia Mountain in Michaux State Forest of Franklin County (DD GPS Coordinates: 39.9089, -77.4783). Follow U. S. Route 30 to Caledonia State Park. Take Route 233 South for about 4½ miles to a pull-off on the right next to the Appalachian Trail crossing. Hike north on the Appalachian Trail for three miles. The Sentinel Rock pillar is on the right.[4]

---

3. Ibid.

4. Although the face found on the rock today is nowhere near as impressive as that in the 1900 *Gettysburg Compiler* photo, park rangers and the gentleman who provided the photos all agreed that, after allowing for over 120 years of weathering and based on their intimate familiarity with the area, that this was indeed the Sentinel Rock of the 1900 Gettysburg Compiler photo! See the chapter titled "Cast Into Stone" in the author's *Pennsylvania Fireside Tales Volume III* for additional details about this unique natural profile.

CHAPTER 3

INDIAN HEAD ROCK

It seems fitting that since our last chapter dealt with a Native American's rocky profile, this next chapter should introduce another rock formation that some say portrays yet another Indian's profile. Similar to why the Indians believed the image of their derelict sentinel appeared on the rocks at current-day Michaux State Forest, there is also an explanation about this next profile, but its provenance is apocryphal. It's no longer known if it came down to us from the local Native Americans or was a story invented by the first white settlers here who found it, but it seems more likely to be of Indian origins since it offers a candid glimpse into their early struggles and tells of another sad incident in the life of the Indians.

Folklore scholars have studied tales like this over the years, and they have recorded numerous examples, with versions surfacing from time to time throughout Pennsylvania and the entire country, for that matter. They are so common that one scholar said that if these tales were all true, the deeds they tell of would have significantly impacted the Native American population! (For more such tales and some historical background on them, see the chapter titled "Maids of the Mist" in the author's *Pennsylvania Fireside Tales Volume 4* and the chapter titled "Faces from the Past" in the author's *Pennsylvania Fireside Tales Volume 6*).

The profile we want to address in this chapter specifically can be found along the Susquehanna River near Catawissa in Columbia County. Locals refer to it as "Profile Rock," but it is also called "Indian Head Rock" by those who know the legend behind it.

Indian Head Rock. (Photo courtesy of American Views Photography & Post Card Company, Bloomsburg, Pennsylvania.)

The entire area through here is steeped in the legend and lore of the Native Americans who settled here first and who left an indelible mark on the area with the names they assigned to their villages and surrounding geographical features. Many would say today that the white settlers who came here unmercifully drove the Indians away but did not eradicate the names the Native Americans left behind. Many of those names survive today, including that of Catawissa.

That name today is an Anglicized version of the name the Shawnee Indians used for their settlement here.[1] In their dialect, the name was "Catawese," but authorities cannot agree on its meaning. Some say it meant "growing fat,"[2] perhaps in reference to the widening of the river at this point, while others say it meant "pure water."[3]

---

1. C. Hale Sipe, *The Indian Chiefs of Pennsylvania*, 748-751.
2. Ibid.
3. John G. Freeze, *History of Columbia County*, 101.

Yet another Pennsylvania "Indian Head." Girty's Rock is named after Indian Trader Simon Girty Senior's son Simon, who was born and raised near Sherman's Creek, Perry County and who became known as the "white savage" after he forsook his white Colonial counterparts and joined the Indians in their ravages of the frontier. (Photo courtesy of E. Schaeffer/J. Rudy.)

In addition to the town, that name has also been assigned to the massive mountain peak that frowns upon it. Catawissa Mountain was once a favorite Indian gathering place owing to the crystal clear pure mountain water that flows copiously and unendingly from a spring on the mountaintop.[4] Today, it remains a favorite destination of Alpine enthusiasts who like to make the ascent, particularly during the hot summer days. Upon reaching the top, many of them, like the Indians once did, enjoy a drink from the same cool waters, but most are unaware of the legends surrounding this spot.

It is said that for many decades a huge gum tree grew beside the spring and that it had been looked upon with great reverence by the Indians.[5]

---

4. J. H. Beers, *Historical and Biographical Annals of Columbia and Montour Counties, Pa.* 188.
5. Ibid.

Although it was a true monarch of the forest due to its immense size, it was also the only one of this kind for miles around. Maybe those things were enough to foster the Indians' admiration of it, but they may have had other reasons or stories associated with it that caused them to hold it in such high esteem.

If so, those reasons and stories are forever lost to us today, as is the gum tree, which was toppled by a high wind years ago.[6] Fortunately, that same fate has not yet befallen that nearby spectacular rock profile on the side of Catawissa Mountain.

After so many decades, this peculiar profile has managed to remain intact and cling to the rock face where it was first seen. Its longevity is surprising, given the fate of a similar stone image that could once be seen in New Hampshire. There the "Old Man of the Mountain" profile was once regarded as a major tourist attraction, but despite efforts to shore it up, it eventually succumbed to the unrelenting forces of nature and crumbled away from the ledge where it had endured for so long.

This undoubtedly will eventually be the fate of the Indian Head formation on Catawissa Mountain. But perhaps its legend is destined to endure longer than that since it tells of love and an untimely end, topics that appeal to true lovers of romance and the reason why devotees of such tales have passed the story down to us today. Their accounts claim the rock face is that of an Indian chief whose spirit is cursed to eternally brood over the place where his daughter snuffed out her own life in response to his cruel actions.

Historical records of this area indicate that at the mouth of Catawissa Creek and on or near the present-day town of Catawissa, there was once an Indian village. The town was home to many Conoys and Delawares who were led by a chief named Lapachpeton.[7]

Not much is known about the chief other than he was a friend of the white man, but the legend that has grown up around his rock profile claims he had an impulsive daughter named Minnetunke who caused him all sorts of grief. At least, that's the way he appears to have felt about it.

It seems that Minnetunke did not find any warriors in her father's tribe that appealed to her romantic nature, but there was a warrior from an

---

6. Ibid.
7. George P. Donehoo, *Indian Villages and Place Names in Pa.*, 145.

The Indian Princess. This "Indian Head" is unusual in that it is that of an Indian woman. Perhaps etched onto the small rock by a contemporary artist rather than by an ancient Native American it nonetheless created quite a stir when found in a cave by workman in the 1840's when cutting out present-day Route 144 through the mountains north of Milesburg in Centre County. (Photo courtesy of E. Schaeffer/J. Rudy.)

enemy tribe across the river who she came to admire and adore. How she met him and then arranged to communicate with him secretly is unknown, but the two lovers agreed on a sheltered meeting place at the edge of a precipice where they could share their love without being seen.

Eventually, perhaps learning of them from some of his trusted spies, her father became suspicious of her late-night excursions. Then one night, he followed her and witnessed the hated enemy warrior in her arms. Enraged, he withdrew a poisoned arrow from his quiver, placed it in his bow, and shot the unsuspecting lover through the heart.

Reeling from pain and surprise, the young warrior toppled over the edge of the nearby cliff and was dashed to pieces when his body hit the rocks below. Seeing her true love's fate, Minnetunke, in a burst of grief and anger, threw herself over that same ledge and suffered a similar fate.[8]

The ancient account does not describe Lapachpeton's reaction upon seeing the consequences of his vindictive actions. However, in an apparent

---

8. Sarah Ann McCool, *Historical Gleanings*, Chap. XLI.

attempt to rectify things, it claims that the gods of love and retribution intervened and cast his spirit into the rock cliff, where he is eternally condemned to look down upon where his daughter and her lover died.

LOCATIONS:

Indian Head Rock can be seen along Route 42 near the village of Catawissa in Columbia County (DD GPS Coordinates: 40.95149, -76.45616).

Girty's Face is located on Second Mountain in Dauphin County, where it frowns upon the village of Dauphin. Photos courtesy of Ernie Schaeffer. For more information on Simon Girty, this hated foe of the white settler, see Sipe's *Indian Wars of Pennsylvania* (pages 317-320) (DD GPS Coordinates: 40.36748, -76.93040).

CHAPTER 4

OLE BULL'S CASTLE

I had been to Ole Bull State Park in the Kettle Creek Valley of Potter County several times in the past, but never once had I attempted to see the stone wall that was painstakingly laid up to prevent the hillside from eroding from the place where a "castle" was to be built for the Park's namesake, a world-famous nineteenth-century violinist from Norway. Some years ago, I saw a picture of that wall and even saw an oil painting of the "castle" supposedly constructed here. So it seemed appropriate that I should include the story of that place in this volume, if for nothing more than to see if those magnificent constructions might still be here today and to share the history and legends surrounding them.

So it was on a beautiful October day in 2020 I revisited Ole Bull State Park, surrounded by the resplendent colors of fall—a day that the great violinist himself would have relished. Invigorated with the anticipation of a successful quest and determined to solve the mysteries I had come here to investigate, I used the park map to start at the head of the Ole Bull Trail, where a nearby monument to Ole Bull can be seen. It had been donated by his home country of Norway and was impressive in both size and design.

The trail was easily found from the monument since it was an old carriage road, and it was not too hard to follow it up toward the mountaintop. But then, in about one-half mile, we came to another trail sign off to the left that marked a much more precipitous side path identified as the "Castle Vista Trail." Despite the overgrown look and the steep climb, the trail's name drew me onto it, but the further I climbed, the more I needed

An artist's portrayal of the castle that was never built. (Painted by local artist C. H. Shearer, it was donated to the Annie Ross Library in Lock Haven by Henry W. Shoemaker, where it hangs yet today.)

to take increasingly deep breaths of the cool and redolent mountain air to keep going.

Then as I kept ascending, I started to think that I would not get a majestic view of any retaining wall if I kept going up. And then, just as I feared, I reached the mountain top and found where the castle and its wall should have been. There I saw a hole in the ground and a cliff face completely overgrown with brush and weeds: no castle, no wall. But it

View of the castle wall from an old postcard showing how the great wall once looked. (Courtesy of the Potter County Historical Society.)

probably should not have been surprising to find things that way since I was not entirely unfamiliar with the story of the failure of Ole Bull's colony just a year after it began.

History relates that in September of 1852, thirty colonists arrived at Ole Bull's envisioned *Walhalla*, or the Norwegian's "Home of the Gods" as he styled it,[1] and where he hoped to induce "hundreds of thousands more to taste the blessings of liberty in that same locality."[2] The area eventually covered over 10,000 acres of land, tracts of which Bull purchased from one John F. Cowan of Williamsport, and gradually the total number of settlers here grew to an estimated count of anywhere from 300 to 800 individuals.[3]

They were an industrious lot, energized by their hopeful visions of success, and they eventually settled in four small towns on Bull's property; all of the villages given Norwegian names as reminders of their home country: Oleona, New Bergen, New Norway, and Walhalla. New Bergen was located at the present-day village of Carter Camp (Cartee Camp); Oleona still exists under that name today; Walhalla was chosen as the site for Bull's splendid castle, and it, along with New Norway, was abandoned when the colony failed in October of 1853.[4]

---

1. Mary E. Welfling, *The Ole Bull Colony in Potter County*, 4.
2. Ibid., 5.
3. Ibid., 4-5.
4. Ibid., 10.

It was an abrupt collapse just over a year after the colonists began building their homesteads on Bull's estate. Illness befell many of them and reduced their numbers, but the final death knell for the Utopian endeavor came when it was learned that Bull's deed for his lands was riddled with "exceptions," which included large parcels that were not included in the purchase and on which colonists had already settled, building homes and planting crops.[5]

Whether it was the fault of Bull's lawyers or a deliberate scam on the part of John Cowan, the legal problems were insurmountable and proved to be the *coup de gras* for Bull's idealistic plans. Maybe it was a combination of incompetent lawyers or the schemes of a con man, but that latter issue could have been decisive, for as one man who knew Cowan later commented, "I would just as soon pick the bait out of a steel trap than have any dealings with him."[6]

Certainly, one of the casualties of the colony's collapse was Ole Bull's "Castle." By then, the colonists had set a huge stone retaining wall on the cliff face that dropped off precipitously in front of the site where the castle was to be built. It was an impressive landmark and stood for decades as a symbol of the Norwegian's dedication and work ethic. But in 1933, the state Forestry Department deemed it unstable and unsafe and directed the Civilian Conservation Corps in the park area to dismantle it and use the stones for their buildings.

The stones for the "castle" itself had also been selected and carried to the castle site, where a large foundation had already been dug as the first step in erecting a magnificent stone edifice that would both honor their benefactor and provide him with a fine residence, befitting someone of his reputation and generosity. That deep hole in the ground can still be seen at the cliff edge today, but a castle was never built, the stones eventually being purchased by local doctor Edward Joerg, who used them as the foundation stones for his own house.[7]

That same house still stands today near the park, and in its dark basement, the stones intended for Ole Bull's Castle support a less noble structure, relegated to a less regal residence. There, hidden in the darkness, they

---

5. Ibid.,11-12.
6. Norman B. Wilkinson, "Ole Bull's New Norway," *Historic Pennsylvania Leaflet #14*, 4.
7. Welfling, op. cit., 14, and information provided by a local resident/Ole Bull Park ranger.

Contemporary view of where the wall once stood. (Photo taken by the author in October 2020.)

will no doubt serve their purpose with the same dignity and durability that they would have provided for Ole Bull's grander home, at least as long as this home continues to stand and serve as a private residence, as it has done to this day.

So traces of Ole Bull's great Walhalla seem to be few and far between. The surviving colonists moved on, many to Wisconsin, Iowa, and Minnesota, but at least one reminder of their former colony survives in the name of Oleona, the town he founded.[8] And also a second in the form of a spring that still bubbles up in the park. The name for the Lyso (or "shining" in Norwegian) Spring evokes thoughts of characters from Norwegian mythology, so images of Valkyries, gnomes, trolls, Vikings and fairies may start appearing in our minds as we stand in that silent spot.

But there is another reminder some say surfaces occasionally, especially in gloomy weather when the wind softly soughs in the hemlocks and white pines. These same stately trees are descendants of those once so dense in this entire northern Pennsylvania forest that it was known as "The Black

---

8. Ibid., 29.

The castle foundation and its historical sign. Today it's just a hole in the ground.

This historical sign at the castle site, which was erected when the retaining wall was still standing.

Forest," a name that reflected that even at midday, the forest floor was as dark as night.⁹

Though that same forest is not as dense today, it still can be dark and foreboding as darkness falls, especially on those nights when leaden-grey clouds float lazily in a moonlit sky, casting dark shadows that flit eerily across the treetops below. It is on nights such as these, some believe, that anyone standing here can, if they listen closely enough, hear the soft, soothing sounds of a violin. But the tune is reportedly melancholy, which seems oddly appropriate when it's recalled how Ole Bull ended his time here.

This account, of unknown origin and veracity, relates that when Ole Bull realized his colony would fail, he dejectedly stood on the edge of the cliff-face in front of his log cabin. As he surveyed that work-in-progress, which was to be his residence until work on his stone "castle" could begin, he perhaps became even more frustrated when he considered what "might have been." Then as darkness fell, he took out his violin and played several sad melodies. As his finale, and in a last act of surrender, he forcefully threw his violin out into the darkness.

The violin, the legendary account relates, may have been a Stradivarius and may have been decorated with diamonds. In either case, it would have been worth a fortune at the time, and those diamonds may still lie at the bottom of the cliff face. No one has ever found them; at least no reports have surfaced to indicate it, but if found, they would provide some evidence that the old tale was a true one.

But are there any facts to support the mystical accounts claiming that strains of phantom music can be heard here from time to time? At least one local author seemed to think so when he claimed that early settlers along Kettle Creek often told a story from the time of the French and Indian War about a detachment of the French Army being ambushed by Indians as they were marching past the site where Ole Bull's castle was supposed to be erected a century later.

With that contingent was a young fifer mortally wounded and left to die. Abandoned by his fleeing comrades, he dragged himself to a nearby spring to quench his thirst with its cool waters, the same spring that Ole Bull would later name the Lyso Spring in honor of the legendary heroes

---

9. Found on DCNR Ole Bull Park web page at dcnr.pa.gov/StateParks/OleBullStatePark.

of his homeland. Here the fifer died, and although his mortal remains became food for the wolf packs that were still prevalent at the time, his love of music kept his spirit alive, and from that time on, it made its presence known by creating ghostly manifestations of the tunes it loved so well.

Or at least that was the popular opinion, as in later years, many travelers following Kettle Creek out of Cross Fork and heading to the Jersey Shore-Coudersport turnpike (present-day Route 44) reported hearing the shrill music of a fife as they passed by the castle site. Neither the sounds of the fife nor the faint strains of Ole Bull's violin have been reported recently, perhaps all silenced by our modern age's skepticism and rational thinking.[10]

> **LOCATION: Ole Bull State Park** is in Susquehannock State Forest of Potter County (DD GPS Coordinates: 41.5359003, -77.7152656). Take Route 144 North into the town of Cross Fork. From there, follow Route 44 North to the park.

---

10. Robert Lyman, Jr., *Forbidden Land, Volume I*, p. 12. His source was apparently Henry W. Shoemaker (See his *Allegheny Episodes*, page 248), which makes the tale apocryphal.

CHAPTER 5

BLUE HILL

Visitors who come to the river town of Northumberland in Northumberland County, and longtime residents of that same place, where the North and West Branches of the Susquehanna River come together, may recall seeing an observation platform along the river and a nearby sign inviting interested parties to ascend the platform's steps to get a closer look at "Shikellamy's Face" which juts out from the edge of the hillside on the opposite shore.

Many people are curious enough to walk up the steps to get a better look at the rocky countenance, but just as many, no doubt, wonder exactly whose face they are viewing on that distant slope. But the answer to that question is not hard to find when the history of this same area is reviewed.

The small hill in question, referred to as "Blue Hill" in colonial times, perhaps named for the blue haze that seems to shroud it when river mists cloak its face, has a unique history. At its summit is a commanding view of the mighty Susquehanna below, and the undulating hills of Northumberland County roll away in the distance, with glimpses of Danville and Sunbury surfacing from that billowing cascade of peaks on clear days.

Perhaps this majestic view and the relative inaccessibility of the summit attracted an eccentric hermit here, who, in 1839, purchased ninety acres of farmland on the summit. According to one popular rumor, John Mason sought the seclusion and obscurity of this site because he was trying to get over a lover who had jilted him and left him with a broken heart. The ascetic bachelor, however, was a man of keen intelligence and a voracious reader.

Table Rock on Blue Hill. (Image from an old postcard.)

Thus his interest in astronomy led him to build an eighteen-by-sixteen-foot observatory here, which he attached to the rock face with strong iron rods. Eventually, he would advertise it as a viewing tower on which people could stand and look out over the dizzying heights below, protected by high railings.

But it would seem only the bravest would venture to do so since Mason's octagonal two-story tower hung at a precarious 22-degree angle off the precipice. When viewed from below, it looked like it would fall off at any moment. Thus its odd slope led locals to refer to it as the "Leaning Tower of Pennsylvania."[1]

---

1. Frederic A. Godcharles, "Today's Story in Pennsylvania History: John Mason, Hermit of Blue Hill, and His Leaning Tower Destroyed, April 22, 1864," *The Tribune*, Scranton, Pa., April 22, 1924.

Painting of John Mason's Tower by local artist M. P. Roush, based on historical descriptions and an 1843 pencil sketch by Mrs. Amelia Donnell. (Used by permission of the artist.)

The eye-catching landmark dangled off the edge of Blue Hill for some twenty-five years, until one April day in 1864, a few railroad men "in a spirit of deviltry" loosened the iron rods that held it to the cliff. The heavy structure broke away, rumbled down Blue Hill, and with a loud crash, bounced onto a log raft that was floating by on the river. It was the end of what was described as "one of the oldest, and one of the most conspicuous, landmarks along the Susquehanna River."[2]

Upon his death some years later, Mason's friends buried him under a spreading chestnut tree several yards in the back of the spot where his "Leaning Tower" once inclined over the waters below. However,

---

2. Ibid.

Shikellamy's Face as it looks today on Blue Hill. The profile is in the middle of the picture just below the power lines.

curiosity-seeking vandals, by their incessant trampling over the gravesite, eventually obliterated it and completely defaced its marble tombstone by chipping off pieces for souvenirs. Thus Mason's friends eventually decided to disinter his remains and bury them under another chestnut tree on a nearby farm.[3]

But although the memory of John Mason's landmark tower is almost forgotten today, rumors persist about him. It is still believed by many, for example, that Mason had accumulated a hoard of silver coins while living on Blue Hill, storing them in barrels and then burying them on the hill near his observatory.[4]

Perhaps many still search for that treasure today, but Mason's spectacular view was, and still is, a magnet for tourists. This was especially true after the magnificent Hotel Shikellamy was built in 1891. The hotel was a popular resort until destroyed by fire in 1898, after which locals still took

---

3. Ibid.
4. Frederic A. Godcharles, "The Hermit of Blue Hill," found at www.treasurenet.com.

Image of Shikellamy's face as highlighted on an old postcard.

picnic lunches to "Table Rock" on the cliff face,[5] but for the most part, the little hill was left in silent slumber until the Pennsylvania Department of Conservation and Natural Resources created Shikellamy State Park here and opened it to the public in 1960.

At that point, another Blue Hill landmark was touted as eye-catching as Mason's tower once had been; the stone profile of Iroquois Chief

---

5. Cindy Inkrote, "Fire destroyed Blue Hill resort," *The Daily Item*, Sunbury, Pa., September 5, 2010.

Another Image of Shikellamy's face. Bronze bust on the wall of the Northumberland County Historical Society in Sunbury.

Shikellamy, the Native American for whom the park was named.[6] The profile is still there, a stark survivor of the ravages of time, so Park visitors can thus still enjoy the view from the summit of Blue Hill and, from a viewing platform on the Northumberland side of the river, gaze out upon that stubborn profile.

That's because the ancient stone silhouette refuses to be obliterated by the same forces of nature that have almost obliterated the remains of the Old Improvement mentioned in the last chapter. Likewise, it has not, like Mason's tower or the Old Man of the Mountain, New Hampshire's famous

---

6. Cindy Inkrote, found at www.stateparks.com/Shikellamy_State_Park_in_Pennsylvania.

rocky cliff profile, fallen away from the cliff face, thereby holding its place as one of the most iconic mountain landmarks in the state. But chief Shikellamy and his Native American brothers have also left other traces of their presence in the area; the names they assigned to these spots and to the related folktales that cling to these same places.

Those familiar with the Indians' legendary domain claim that they looked upon Blue Hill as a fearsome place, believing that evil spirits dwelt in the forbidding cavern that yawned at the base of the rock clefts. They even named the place *Otzinachson*, or "The Demon's Den," and gave it a wide berth when steering their birch bark canoes past it.[7]

There is another spot near here that was also held in some reverence, and perhaps as much superstitious awe, by those same Native Americans, and that is the small island in the river we refer to today as The Isle of Que. It, too, has an interesting history, especially the speculation about the origin of its name and a story about how it featured in a so-called "dream contest" between Conrad Weiser, the Indian agent for the Penn family, and chief Shikellamy.

The Native American presence in this area was well established when the first Moravian settlers came here in the 18th century; the Indians' much-used Penns Creek Path, a prominent feature that extended from Frankstown, present-day Blair County in the southwest, through New Berlin, and ending in present-day Northumberland.[8]

And the seat of chief Shikellamy, the vice-regent of the Iroquois who came here in 1727, also a well-known place along the West Branch. Shikellamy's Town, as it was referred to, could be found about half a mile below present-day Milton until Shikellamy relocated it to present-day Sunbury, or "Shamokin," as the Indians called it, in 1738.[9]

But it appears that for decades the local Indians had another place of special significance to them as well, a place of internment for their dead. And that place was the aforementioned Isle of Que, which, we know from historical records, was indeed an isle of the dead. As Meginness in his *History of the West Branch Valley* records, "The general burial ground of

---

7. John F. Meginness, *History of Lycoming County*, 45.
8. Paul A. W. Wallace, *Indian Paths of Pennsylvania*, 126.
9. C. Hale Sipe, *Indian Chiefs of Pennsylvania*, 122.

View of the Isle of Que as seen from across the river at Fisher's Ferry.

the Indians was on the Isle of Que, near its southern extremity, and must contain hundreds, nay thousands, of bodies; for the skeletons have been found over a quarter of a mile in length and breadth. In digging for the foundation of Christian Fisher's house, seven skeletons were found. Others were dug up at various places between the afore-mentioned points."[10]

This historical account leads to yet another piece of historical evidence that seems to support the idea that the island's name is based on the fact that it is truly an "Isle of the Dead." Evidence can be found in the journals of Conrad Weiser, the highly-respected Indian agent for the Penn family, who kept a daily record of his travels among the Indians. There is an entry in Weiser's journal for July 29, 1745, in which he describes being informed by Mohawk Indians about a tragic event that once befell their tribe. It reads in part as follows (spelling is as exactly found in Weiser's journal): "The dead cry was everywhere, Que, Que, Que!"[11]

---

10. John F. Meginness, *Otzinachson*, 101.
11. Conrad Weiser, *Papers, 1741-1783*, Collection 700, Historical Society of Pennsylvania.

View of Fisher's Ferry across the river as seen from the Isle of Que today.

Weiser's comment does lend credence as to why the Isle of Que is named as such, and it also seems to debunk a local legend that was once entertained as a true story by those who love the tales that cling to the West Branch Valley—the aforementioned tale about a so-called dream contest between Shikellamy and Conrad Weiser.

Early missionaries among the Native American tribes of New England and Pennsylvania also kept journals of their travels, several of them noting that the Indians generally held dreams in special reverence, believing that they held the key to the overall health of mind and body. "It would be cruelty, nay, murder, not to give a man the subject of his dreams, for such a refusal might cause his death!"[12]

Conrad Weiser was reminded of this Native American belief one day in 1754 when his friend Shikellamy expressed great admiration for a new rifle the Indian agent was carrying, and the very next day told Weiser that on the previous night, he had dreamt that Weiser had given it to him as a

---

12. Paul A. W. Wallace, *Indians in Pennsylvania*, 92-93.

gift. Acutely aware of how the Indian regarded such dreams, Weiser felt he had no choice but to give the rifle to the canny chief.

But the next day, he turned the tables on his Oneida friend when he told him that he had dreamed that Shikellamy had given him the Isle of Que as a gift. The legendary account goes on to say that Shikellamy gave his friend Weiser the real estate of his dream but also cautioned him to "let us never dream again!"[13]

Although the account of the "dream contest" between Shikellamy and Conrad Weiser sounds plausible, it appears to be nothing more than a legend since similar tales could once be heard in New York, South Carolina, and Georgia.[14] Then too, it hardly seems plausible that Shikellamy would turn over a sacred Indian burial ground like the Isle of Que to a white man in so flippant a manner. Nonetheless, the account keeps alive the memory of two great figures in Pennsylvania's Colonial history and also enhances the mystique that clings to this Pennsylvania landmark and Blue Hill to this day.

NOTE: See the chapter titled "Faces From the Past" in the author's *Pennsylvania Fireside Tales Volume VI* for more details on the tales mentioned in this chapter.

LOCATIONS:

Blue Hill is located within Shikellamy State Park in Union County at the confluence of the North and West Branches of the Susquehanna River near Sunbury, Northumberland County (DD GPS Coordinates: 40.9361976, -76.616345). Follow route 15 south from Lewisburg until you reach a stop light for the bridge to Sunbury. Turn left at the stoplight and continue along the river, where you can see the cliffs. Continue along the river until you see the sign for Shikellamy State Park.

The Isle of Que lies in the West Branch of the Susquehanna River just outside Selinsgrove, Snyder County (DD GPS Coordinates: 40.806244, -76.860708). Continue on Route 15 South from Sunbury and into Selinsgrove. Get onto North Water Street, follow to East Pine St., turn left onto East Pine Street, and cross the bridge onto the Isle of Que.

---

13. Ibid.
14. Ernest W. Baughman, *Type and Motif Index*, 340.

CHAPTER 6

KING WI-DAAGH'S GRAVE[1]

To lovers of Pennsylvania's storied past, the name Henry W. Shoemaker holds a preeminent place in the annals of the state's folklore. Unfortunately, however, even though he deserves credit for being among the first, if not the first, collectors of the Keystone State's treasure house of legends and folktales, his reputation has been tarnished by the realization that many, if not all, of his tales, are either highly-embellished versions of the stories he heard from his sources or complete fabrications from his fertile imagination. In fact, in recalling him to me, one of his early acquaintances, who knew the man well, noted that "once he picked up his pen, it got away from him!"[2]

Nonetheless, it's an interesting exercise to analyze Shoemaker's stories to decide if there are any "kernels of truth" upon which they are based. When doing so, you eventually realize that, in many cases, there are nuggets of history embedded in his tales, no matter how far-fetched the stories themselves may sound. And one of Shoemaker's most fantastic accounts may be the story he called "King Wi-daagh's Spell (a story of Antes Fort Mountain)," which appeared in his volume titled *Tales of the Bald Eagle Mountains*. But examining that unusual romance for historical accuracy and from a present-day perspective proves interesting.[3]

---

1. This article was written by the author for *The Hemlock*, a publication of the English Department at Lock Haven University. It appeared in their Spring 2015 issue (Volume 9, Issue 2), pp 6–11.
2. Samuel W. Bayard, interviewed December 26, 1977.
3. Henry W. Shoemaker, *Tales of the Bald Eagle Mountains*, 137.

Shoemaker begins his legend as follows: "It was the unvarying custom, and perhaps the chief peculiarity of King Wi-daagh, the last ruler of the Susquehanna Indians, that any of his subjects who happened to lay eyes on him, must return and see him again one year from the date. He imagined this instilled a proper respect for his exalted station, especially when the person who had looked at him would have to travel two hundred miles through forests drifted with snow to repeat the performance. If he but knew it, his subjects came to "hate the sight of him" for this very reason. But he had other faults.

"As a financier, he was a failure, even for an Indian. His bargain with the Proprietary Government in September 1700, a century after his great ancestor Pipsisseway's military triumphs, when he deeded the fertile Otzinachson Valley to the Penn family for a few trinkets and a bale of English goods, will stand out as the most one-sided land deals in history. Though he ever regretted the sale, he kept it mostly to himself, which is to his credit. But to the day of his death, he was pompous and overbearing to his kind, exaggerating trifles and glossing over important events in life. As long as his followers returned the following year after seeing him, he was satisfied. To put people into trouble seemed to be his chief delight.

"Wi-daagh's favorite walk was from his palace, which consisted of a many-roomed cavern near the source of Antes Creek, along the stream, and thence westward to a small spring, where in his youth he had met clandestinely an Indian maid of inferior birth.

"Along the creek was the favorite pathway for Indians traveling north or south, and he invariably met troops of victims on every stroll. Much as they originally revered this august symbol of royalty, they hated the idea of having to come back a year from the date of their chance meetings with him."

Shoemaker adds many more apocryphal historic details to his narrative as he continues, but he once again reiterates the point that anyone "unlucky enough to have crossed the Susquehanna, and met the King at his spring" found themselves a year later back at that same spring as though drawn there by dark, mysterious forces. Shoemaker also notes that anyone who tried to avoid this annual rendezvous would be rounded up and burned at the stake, a practice which continued until a "delegation of Quakers from the Proprietary Government" learned of the practice and strongly recommended that the chief abandon this cruel form of persuasion.

"He reluctantly did so," says Shoemaker, but "he lived the balance of his life a broken-hearted man," mourning his loss of power, which hastened his untimely death at his "seat" along Antes Creek. He was buried in "full warrior's regalia," so states Shoemaker, and interred "on the present-day Lochabar Estate" near the deep blue spring that bears his name today.

Of course, Shoemaker could not resist turning his tale into a ghost story, which is understandable considering the dark vale surrounding the spring yet today and the eerie mists that shimmer and dance over Antes Creek in the fall of the year. It's a perfect setting for a ghost tale, and Shoemaker claimed that "King Wi-daagh's ghost was as unhappy as the living tenement had been and had not been in his grave a week before he acquired the habit of taking midnight strolls through the Gap to the small spring at the foot of the upper mountain."

And, said Shoemaker, it was believed that Wi-daagh's ghost would sometimes appear from in the back of a large oak tree alongside the Antes Creek path or in the light of campfires built by Indians who "were unlucky enough to build them" along that same path. The apparition would hold out its hand as though trying to give something to those who beheld it and then "sink back into the gloom and vanish." It was, writes Shoemaker, a curse for those who saw the chief's ghost, for they too found themselves compelled to return to Antes Gap a year later, and so the Indians "took especial care" not to warn the white man of the ghost and the spell it cast on those who saw it. In this way, the Indians, claimed Shoemaker, would "have the last laugh on their white conquerors."

Quite a story, to be sure, and no reports of Wii-daagh's ghost have surfaced since Shoemaker's time, at least none known to this writer, but a visit to Wi-daagh's Spring along Antes Creek today does prove interesting as far as other aspects of Shoemaker's account. You see, the Lochabar Estate, located at the foot of the Bald Eagle Mountain in Nippenose Township, Lycoming County, and near the village of Antes Fort, is perhaps not referred to as such anymore, but it still holds the same landmarks that were there in Shoemaker's day, including the old oak tree and the spring named after the infamous Indian chief.

Widaagh's gravesite near Lochabar.

    The estate is private land, and permission should be obtained before venturing down the gravel road that leads back to Wi-daagh's spring, but the lady I met on the road when driving back to get permission to see the landmark one day turned out to be the owner of the property and, despite my incursion, was very affable and friendly. In fact, when I asked her if she knew the legend of Wi-daagh, she said that, of course, she did and that she had even named the large dog she had in her truck with her King Wi-daagh.

    She then asked me if I knew where the chief's gravesite was located, and when I said it had been fifteen years since I had been there, she kindly directed me to the inconspicuous site. I followed a narrow dirt trail alongside Antes Creek, all the while enjoying the beautiful fall splendor around me and being calmed by the peaceful sound of the waters of the creek as they cascaded over the rocks in the creek bed alongside the path until I saw the gravesite and the vertical shaft of stone that marks the old chief's final resting place. Satisfied by my discovery, I retraced my steps, hoping to find the disgraced chief's spring next.

A close-up view of Widaagh's gravestone.

In another reference, Shoemaker described the spring and the land around it as the "favorite camping ground of King Widaagh, the Indian chief." However, Shoemaker also mentions that near the spring is "one of the pillars of the old State Capitol at Harrisburg, destroyed by fire in 1896" and erected here in 1900 by the late George L. Sanderson, owner of the estate at that time, to commemorate the 200th anniversary of Widaagh's treaty with the Penn family.[4] We soon saw the impressive obelisk, but it was the inscription on it that drew us closer and which described the history of this beautiful spot.

---

4. Henry W. Shoemaker, *Eldorado Found*, 68.

Widaagh's deep blue emerald spring at Lochabar.

"Wi-daagh, King of the Susquehanna Indians, whose wigwam was here. Executed treaty with Wm. Penn Sept 13, 1700, conveying Susquehanna River and lands adjoining in consideration of a parcel of English goods. Erected Sept 13, 1900."

After taking pictures of the pillar and of the beautiful blue spring nearby, I felt it was a fitting end to my visit to Lochabar, which, also according to Shoemaker, is the name of a small lake in Scotland that signifies "Lake of the Horns," so-named because "so many deer shed their antlers here."[5]

Today Lochabar is one of the 16 ward management areas of the Highland Council of Scotland, but there seems to be some debate about the name's true meaning. Scottish sources say the name means the 'lake of horns,' with the "tradition being that the deer, in the rutting season, fought about this lake and lost their horns."[6]

However, some say that this definition is "fanciful." Other historical searches, on the other hand, confirmed that Wi-daagh is not a fanciful name and that the old chief was indeed a very real person.

---

5. Ibid.
6. Sir John Sinclair, *The Statistical Accounts of Scotland,* Vol. 8, 430.

The Capitol Pillar at Lochabar.

The fact that locals still point out his gravesite is, of course, suggestive, but the fact that his name cannot be found in prominent Colonial histories like the *Frontier Forts of Pennsylvania*, C. Hale Sipe's *Indian Wars of Pennsylvania*, or Hannah's *Wilderness Trail* raises some doubts. However, in *Volume 1* of the Pennsylvania Archives (page 133) there is included the wording of a September 13th, 1700, land purchase agreed upon by two Indian chiefs occupying the lands at that time and by James Logan and other representatives of William Penn.

In that agreement, the Indians conveyed "all the Said River Susquehannagh, and all the Islands therein, and all the Land Situate lying upon both sides of the said River . . . in Consideration of a Parcel of English Goods."

The two chiefs whose names and whose "marks" appear on the agreement are "*Andaggy* (alias *Junkquagh*)" and "*Widaagh* (alias *Orytyagh*)."

This document confirms that Widaagh was a real person and was the signer of the Penns' infamous purchase of the Susquehanna lands. Further checking of Sipe's *Indian Chiefs of Pennsylvania* reveals that the Indian chiefs Widaagh and Junkquagh were "Kings or Sachems of the Susquehanna Indians."[7]

It is also noted here that on October 7th, 1701, Oretyagh, with other Indian chiefs representing the Conestogas and Shawnees, came to Philadelphia to bid farewell to their friend William Penn shortly before his final departure for England.

"The parties parted in peace and mutual respect, with the chiefs expressing great satisfaction in a law that they were told would be passed shortly that would prevent their being abused by the selling of rum among them. Oretyagh spoke for them all when he said that his people had "long suffered from the ravages of the rum traffic" and that he now hoped for redress, believing that they would "have no reason for complaint of this matter in the future."[8]

It seems evident from the historical record that, since another chief also signed the purchase agreement, Shoemaker unfairly saddled Widaagh solely with the blame for selling the Susquehanna lands to William Penn "for a parcel of English goods." A second chief also signed the deed and deserves some blame. As to Shoemaker's contention that Widaagh's spirit is restless, still lamenting over a poor real estate deal and occasionally appearing to those unlucky enough to see it, it would seem that that is a moot point today.

The reason is that the defamed chief's soul should be content in the knowledge that its resting place is still being preserved and that its memory is still held in respect, as evidenced by the Indian tobacco ceremony for the dead that is sometimes conducted here by the present owners of the estate or by present-day Native Americans.[9]

---

7. C. Hale Sipe, *The Indian Chiefs of Pennsylvania*, 76.
8. Ibid., 74 ff.
9. It is interesting to note that it was a long-held local belief that King Widaagh's ghost haunted the "Enchanted Spring" at Lochabar long before Henry Shoemaker published his story in 1912. See Uriah Cummings 1900 colorful work titled "The Song of U-RI-ON-TAH" (particularly pages 167 and 426 ff).

LOCATION: Wiidaagh's grave is along Antes Creek in Lycoming County, about two miles southeast of Jersey Shore (DD GPS Coordinates: 41.1917403, -77.2238586). From the village of Antes Fort, continue on Route 44 South until you come to a private lane off to the right near the foot of the downgrade. Turn right onto the road, which parallels Antes Creek on the right side of the dirt road. This private road leads back to a part of George Sanderson's former Lochabar estate and his "Little Lochabar," a fine cottage he constructed for his fishing friends. Permission should be obtained before visiting Wiidaagh's grave along the creek and the emerald spring in front of the house. See Chapter #12 in this volume for more on the much larger Lochabar manor house and its veritable "skeleton in the closet!"

CHAPTER 7

HOODOO

Geologists have jokingly called them "nature's hilarious accidents," but the more refined scientific title they use when referring to them is "PBRs," or Precariously Balanced Rocks. However, common folks have coined their names for these unusual rock formations over the years. Their titles vary from area to area, with "fairy chimneys," "tent rocks," "hoodoos," and "earth pyramids" being just a few of the variations. But regardless of the name given to them, they attract attention because of their seemingly impossible balancing act or because their shapes seem so unnatural.[1]

PBRs also appeal to geologists because they are seismic indicators, or "reverse seismometers" in the parlance of the geologist. That's because they indicate the intensity of past earthquakes, not predictors of future ones. The fact that they are still standing proves that any past seismic rumbles were not strong enough to topple them.[2]

There are many such PBR formations worldwide, including some spectacular ones here in the Keystone State, and in this chapter, we'll introduce several of them, beginning with one of the most accessible; the Balanced Rock in Trough Creek State Park of Huntingdon County.

Named for the Great Trough Creek that cuts through Terrace Mountain and drains into Raystown Lake, today's park area and the surrounding land was once inhabited by Native Americans. But these sons of the forest

---

1. Sabrina Imbler, "Why Scientists fall for Precariously Balanced Rocks," January 9, 2020, www.Atlasobscura.com.
2. Ibid.

The Balanced Rock, located in Trough Creek State Park.

were gradually displaced when settlers came here, attracted by the prospect of water power that could be harnessed from the fast-flowing waters of Trough Creek Gorge.

Thus the area became the home to several mills of different sorts, several iron forges, and Reuben Trexler's famous Paradise iron furnace. But the vagaries of commerce eventually spelled doom for this thriving commercial center in 1856, and even the Civil War's demands for iron products could not revive it enough to enable it to recover and survive. It was not until 1933 that the area found new life once again.

It was in that post-Depression year that the boys of the Civilian Conservation Corps (CCC) arrived here and built CCC Camp Paradise Furnace,

Another view of the Balanced Rock.

which served as their headquarters while they planted trees, built roads, blazed trails, and erected recreational facilities in this part of Rothrock State Forest. It was their camp and their work that eventually became the state park that is enjoyed by so many today.[3]

The 531-acre park is a natural wonderland, not only because of the work of the CCC but also because of the many natural wonders that can be found here. Among them are Raven Rocks, said to be the inspiration for Edgar Allen Poe's poem named after those same birds and the ice mine, with its frigid temperatures noticeable even during the hottest days of summer. The colorful natural rainbows of Rainbow Falls are a delight to see as well, as are the vibrant colors of the Copperas Rocks.[4]

But the most spectacular natural wonder amongst the grand scenery that is to be found here is the Balanced Rock. Celebrated far and wide for its balancing act, this PBR looks like it could, at any moment, slide off the edge of the cliff face to which it so tenaciously clings. But it has maintained

3. Pennsylvania Department of Conservation and Natural Resources, "2011 Recreational Guide for Trough Creek State Park."
4. Ibid.

A precarious balancing act along the Standing Stone Trail.

that tenuous hold for thousands of years, and until erosion finally causes it to fall, it may continue to stay there for centuries to come.

The chapter titled "The Three Sisters" describes several other unusual Huntingdon County rock formations that can be found along the Standing Stone Trail in the rugged Rocky Ridge Natural Area. Among these are several balanced rock formations, and one of these, like its counterpart in Trough Creek State Park, seems poised to topple from its precarious perch along the mountaintop if it were not for a single tree that seemingly holds it in place!

The PBRs on Rocky Ridge are not as accessible as the Balanced Rock at Trough Creek State Park, but Pulpit Rock in Huntingdon County and Dinosaur Rock in Lebanon County are much more so. Both of these stacks of barely-balanced rock towers can be seen from township roads that pass right by them, but this, at least in the case of Dinosaur Rock, gives vandals a chance to exhibit their callous artistic talents in the form of spray-painted graffiti upon the rocks.

This shameful indifference to nature's artwork is especially visible on Dinosaur Rock, where spray-painted symbols and initials have ruined that

Another PBR held in place by a single tree, located in the Rocky Ridge Natural Area.

natural wonder. It can only be hoped that these social miscreants are someday made to pay for their defilements and also scrub them off the rocks. The accompanying photo of Dinosaur Rock is a photo-shopped version in which I have removed the spray-painted "artwork." Thankfully Pulpit Rock in Huntingdon County has not yet been the target of similar vandalism, despite the fact that it can be viewed as another Dinosaur type rock.

In the next chapter, we will look at even more spectacular Pennsylvania PBRs, which are much harder to find and require seasoned hiking skills and stamina to reach but are well worth the effort to get to them.

More balanced rocks in Rocky Ridge.

Dinosaur Rock (Photoshopped to remove the graffiti).

The author at Pulpit Rock. It could also be aptly named Dinoasaur Rock!

LOCATIONS:

Trough Creek State Park is in Rothrock State Forest near Raystown Lake and the village of Entriken in Huntingdon County (DD GPS Coordinates: 40.3286879, -78.1313961). From Huntingdon in Huntingdon County, drive 16 miles south on Route 26, then near the village of Entriken, follow Pa. Route 994 east to the park entrance.

Rocky Ridge Natural Area is located in Rothrock State Forest near Martin's Gap of Huntingdon County (DD GPS Coordinates: 40.3390, -77.5093). From State College, take Route 26 south to the village of McAleveys Fort. About a mile out of town, you will come to a stop sign, where you'll turn left to stay on Route 26. Continue on Route 26 for about five miles until you see Martin's Gap Road on the left. Turn left onto Martin's Gap Road and continue about a mile until you see a bridge on the left. Cross the bridge and make an immediate right. Drive on this road for approximately one mile, and at a Y intersection, bear right onto Frew Road. There is a parking area for the trailhead leading onto the Standing Stone Trail and into Rocky Ridge Natural Area.

Dinosaur Rock is in State Game Lands #145, in Lebanon County, just north of the turnpike (DD GPS Coordinates: 40.2284265, -765055233). From the village of Colebrook, Lebanon County, follow Route 241 South and look for a parking area on the left. Dinosaur Rock is in the woods on the opposite side of the road to the right.

Pulpit Rock can be found near the village of Donation in Huntingdon County (DD GPS Coordinates: 40.5906255, -778727769). Follow Route 26 South from State College. After passing through the village of Jackson Corner in Huntingdon County, the first road off to the right is Wesley Chapel Road. Turn right onto this road and follow until you see Pulpit Rock on the right.

CHAPTER 8

TOWERING ABOVE THE REST

Perhaps, judging from the vandalism that is inflicted upon natural wonders that don't require strenuous efforts to reach them, like Dinosaur Rock noted in the previous chapter, it is fortunate that Umbrella Rock and Tomahawk Rock, both in Elk County and Ticklish Rock in Sullivan County are so inaccessible. Of all the Precariously Balanced Rocks (PBRs) in Pennsylvania, these three are probably the finest and almost as fine as those in other states.

Umbrella Rock is unique enough that it is addressed in the chapter of the same name in *Volume 1* of this series. The two others mentioned in the preceding paragraph could have been included in the previous chapter on precariously balanced rocks but are, in my opinion, in a class of their own. Hence, this chapter.

Tomahawk Rock is located on State Game Lands 44, just off the Clarion-Little Toby Trail and along the Clarion River near Ridgway. It is not easy to find unless you get a local guide to take you there. It also requires a steep one-mile climb over some rocky patches to get to the Indian Rocks formation in which it stands. Even once you are there at the Indian Rocks, Tomahawk Rock is not easy to locate without further searching. But I had made up my mind to get to it because of its mammoth size and a hint that there may be a phantom bobcat that haunts the place.

Tomahawk Rock, located in Elk County.

I was a bit dumbfounded when I first saw a picture of Tomahawk Rock, sent to me by an Elk County friend. There on the face of the rocks was a faint image, much lighter than the rock face itself, of a bobcat. The image appeared to show the outline of its head, ears, body and chest, with its front legs seemingly placed firmly on a rock in front of the cat. My friend had not noticed the image in the photo and was unsure what it was. I suspected a natural explanation would be the answer, but I wanted to see for myself.

So it was that I made the 2.4-mile up-and-back trek on the Indian Rocks Trail one fine day in May of 2021. My guide was much younger and in much better shape, but she let me catch up when I fell behind, and we finally got to the rocks. The huge monolith with the head of the tomahawk sitting on top was as impressive as I had anticipated, and staring right back at me was the ghostly image of the bobcat.

A closer look confirmed my suspicion that the phantom bobcat was nothing more than discoloration on the rocks, but it was still impressive

Mounted specimen of a Bobcat at Greenwood Furnace State Park. Compare with image of the phantom bobcat seen on Tomahawk Rock.

Another mounted specimen of a bobcat as can be found at Leonard Harrison State Park, Tioga County.

The author at Tomahawk Rock and its phantom bobcat.

and must have been a source of wonder to the Indians who sometimes used these titanic rocks for shelter as they traveled along their trade routes through this area.

There were several prominent Indian paths through what is now the Allegheny National Forest and the Clarion River system, which, in addition to the Allegheny River, is the only other river in this Pennsylvania Wilds area that has been federally designated as part of the National Wild and Scenic Rivers System.[1]

The main Indian paths through the Clarion River System, according to Paul A. W. Wallace, in his *Indian Paths of Pennsylvania*, included the Frankstown-Venango Path, the Goschgoschink Path, and, to the west, the Great Catawba War Path and the Venango-Chinklacamoose Path.[2] As time passed, those Indian paths gave way to bridle paths and wagon roads, and then eventually to motor highways and railroad trackways, so that the pathways of the Indian have been obliterated.

Today there is even little evidence of the railways that crisscrossed the forests here, with former railroad stations like Croyland being little more than ghost towns that lie abandoned in the dark forest that broods over them.[3] And eventually, the spectacular natural rocky wonders that survive, despite their precarious balancing acts, will become nothing more than ghostly memories as well, the forces of erosion that created them in the first place also being the cause of their eventual demise. And nowhere is there more suggestive evidence that this will indeed be the fate of our PBRs than the clues provided by the PBR natives of Sullivan County have named Ticklish Rock.

Ticklish Rock has to be rated as Pennsylvania's premiere PBR; its fantastic stacking is a marvel to behold. Since it is not leaning on the cliffs beside it, nor is it supported in any way except by the delicately balanced position of the rocks themselves, the chances that this ten to fifteen-foot-high pinnacle will stay that way seem very slim indeed, like a mere puff of breath would be enough to topple it over.

The fact that it has not been toppled over by strong blasts of winter wind or by leonine bursts of March weather is due in part because it is tucked safely along a cliff in Shrewsbury Township of Sullivan County.

---

1. Paul A. W. Wallace, *Indian Paths of Pennsylvania*, pp. 27, 56, 61, 174.
2. John D. Imhof, *Elk County, A Journey Through Time*, p. 38.
3. Ibid.

Ticklish Rock, located on Pocono Knob in Sullivan County.

A view of the Muncy Valley as seem from Ticklish Rock, Sullivan County.

A close-up view of Ticklish Rock, Pennsylvania's premier PBR, showing just how unsteady it appears to be.

Part of the great Catskill Formation found in Pennsylvania and New York State, the rocky escarpment of sedimentary sandstone forms a protective shield for the teetering rocks that hug it closely but which do not touch it in the slightest way.

The cliffs, and Ticklish Rock itself, are products of the constant weathering that has slowly worn away the sandstone rocks except, by some fiendish quirk of nature, the pedestal on top of which an enormous rock maintains a fitful perch. The whole ensemble looks like a large upright hammer, with the hammerhead being a huge rock eight feet long, six feet wide, and

A close-up of Ticklish Rock from an old postcard. I would have been able to get this same photo if I'd rappelled down the cliff face beside the rock, but my lady, and my friend who was with us, discouraged it. I finally decided not to risk life and limb since I satisfied myself it was still there. Also I had been able to get some good photos from above. At age 76 I decided not to risk injuring myself; there are other places to explore yet!

about three feet high. That impressive structure is in and by itself enough to elicit wonder in anyone who looks upon it, but it has yet another quality that makes it even more odd.

Those who have tried it, and it would seem the attempts have occurred for over a hundred years since Ticklish Rock has had that name for as long as anyone can remember, claim that if the rock pedestal is pushed, even if slightly, the whole formation will quiver, just like someone would do if they were being tickled.[4]

---

4. Pennsylvania Department of Internal Affairs (1939), "Ticklish Rock – One of State's curious formations," Pennsylvania Department of Internal Affairs Monthly Bulletin 7, #11, pp 3-4.

The author and some "William Penn Trees," Forest Cathedral Natural Area, Cook Forest.

Either those attempts have been gentle, or there have been so few of them because the rock had never toppled over, even when a daredevil somehow climbed up and perched on top of the hammerhead (at least a picture of that foolhardy person has been circulated on the Internet). It is hoped that future generations will not be so cavalier about their handling and treatment of the rock and will show it the respect it well deserves, thus preserving it for future generations until the time comes when Mother Nature decides it's time to bring the show to a close once and for all.[5]

> LOCATIONS:
>
> **Tomahawk Rock** is in State Game Lands #44, near Ridgway, Elk County (DD GPS Coordinates: 41.345617, -78.8164192). From Ridgway, follow Route 949 southwest, approximately 7 miles toward the village of Portland Mills. Just before coming to a bridge spanning railroad tracks (if you come to a second bridge spanning Toby Creek, you've gone too far), turn left on a dirt road leading to State Game Commission buildings. Follow this road about a mile to those buildings, and then follow the road to the right of them to the Little Toby/Clarion River Rails to Trails parking area. Park here and follow a bike trail about a half mile until you see the Indian Rock trail sign. Follow it up the mountain about ½ mile to the rocks. Tomahawk Rock is hidden behind the large rocks in the front.
>
> **Ticklish Rock** can be found on a private hunting preserve near World's End State Park and the village of Tivoli, in Shrewsbury Township, Sullivan County. Hikers to Ticklish Rock are permitted on Sundays. Otherwise, permission is needed (DD GPS Coordinates: 41.35063, -76.648). From the village of Muncy in Sullivan County, follow Route 405 North to Picture Rocks. There, get onto Route 220 North and follow to the village of Tivoli. Drive through Tivoli and continue for about 1½ miles to a dirt road to the left. There is no road sign for the road, but later signs identify it as Deer Lake Road. Turn left on this road and follow it for about four miles to a stop sign at State Route 3005 on the right (the stop sign is hard to see). Turn right on this road (Ticklish Rock Road) and follow to a pullover just before a gated hunting lodge. Follow the trail up the mountain to Ticklish Rock.

---

5. We could hardly end this chapter without mentioning other natural wonders that "tower above the rest." In this case, the wonders in question are not rocks but trees that can be found in the Forest Cathedral Natural Area in Pennsylvania's Cook Forest State Park. This magnificently preserved forest contains one of Pennsylvania's largest, if not the largest, old-growth forests. Home to some of the tallest tree species in the Northeastern United States, the area has appropriately been referred to as "The Land of Giants" and is registered as a National Natural Landmark. Many of the white pine and eastern hemlock titans growing here are close to 200 feet tall, and some have a circumference of almost 14 feet. The larger ones are considered over 300 years old, and trees of this age were referred to as "William Penn trees" by early lumbermen since they dated back to William Penn's founding of Pennsylvania. Today there remains a notable relic named the Longfellow Pine. It holds the record as the tallest tree in the northeastern United States. Standing at 183.6 feet tall, it has a circumference of 11.1 feet at breast height. (Preceding information found on a sign standing at the entrance to the "Big Trees" section of Forest Cathedral Natural Area in Cook Forest State Park, and also in an article titled "Cook vs. Mohawk: Where the Tall Trees Grow," appearing in the Winter 2013 issue of *American Forests Magazine*).

CHAPTER 9

A HEAVENLY PATH

It might be said that since we "gave the devil his due" in our *Volume 1* chapter titled "Infernal Evidence" and in yet another titled "Satan's Handwork," which will appear in *Volume 3*, we should have at least one chapter devoted to the natural wonders that reflect the heavenly realm as well. Several places in our Pennsylvania mountains can be mentioned, and this chapter highlights some of them.

Although there appear to be no cross-shaped Pennsylvania natural rocks, nor any resembling a heavenly personage like an angel or Christ himself, there are natural formations and images that have reminded some folks of things religious. So let's take a heavenly path through the mountains (even though any mountain path is a heavenly experience for me) to discover some of them.

There's no better place to start in that regard than the towering piles that so vividly reminded people of a pastor's altar or pulpit that they named them such. Rothrock's Rock, also called Pulpit Rock, is one remarkable example, and will be included as a separate chapter in our forthcoming *Pennsylvania Mountain Landmarks Volume 3*. In this volume, Pulpit Rock along Whitechapel Road in Huntingdon County (mentioned in our "Hoodoo" chapter) is yet another remarkable monolith of similar character that can be seen near Round Island Station of Clinton County.

Known locally as Altar Rock, it has also been referred to by various writers as Pulpit Rock, Chimney Rock, Steeple Rock and Nelson's Rock. This impressive natural wonder towers over those who find their way to

A HEAVENLY PATH

View of the Sinnemahoning from atop Altar Rock.

My late wife standing at Altar Rock with the plywood Indians standing on the rock.

Antique illustration titled "Men on a cliff in the Alleghany Mountains." The scene depicts a heavenly path indeed. Artist and date unknown. Eerily similar to the scene at Altar Rock along the Sinnemahoning Creek in Clinton County! (Source: Lycoming County Pennsylvania Historical Society Journal Volume LVII Winter 2021–2022.)

it. Rising to a height of sixty feet, it supports a flat rock measuring ten by twelve feet.

When I visited there in 1993, there was a colorful plywood figure of an Indian standing upright on the slab, placed there by the current owners in commemoration of an Indian legend that has clung to this spot for centuries. Although of doubtful authenticity since it came from the facile pen of early folklorist Henry W. Shoemaker, the legend bears repeating since the Indian figure was there in 1993 and may still be there. Hence it may continue to tweak the curiosity of those who venture here today.

Altar Rock was a favorite viewing spot for the Indians since it provided a clear view of traffic on the Sinnemahoning Creek below, quietly flowing through the breathtaking wilds of present-day Bucktail State Park Natural Area. Supposedly, according to Shoemaker, in the first quarter of the eighteenth century, a fiery Indian brave, resentful of their intrusions, killed a French trapper near here. Later the Indian, whose name, Shoemaker states, was "Two Pines," was shot by the French Trapper's friends when they saw Two Pines standing on Altar Rock and shouting in defiance at them.

Years later, two white pine trees, seemingly growing from solid rock with no nutrient sources, sprouted from Altar Rock as though commemorating the young Indian who died there. Knowing that legend, I was not surprised when I found the plywood Indian standing on Altar Rock the day my wife and I hiked up to the iconic spot. The current owners later explained that they placed the figure there to remind people of the old legend, no matter how historically inaccurate it may be.[1]

There is another Altar Rock with a more solid claim to that name; a name not based on any legendary claims, but on the historically-documented proof that it was once used as a place of worship. Located in Scripture Rocks Heritage Park near Brookville in Jefferson County, this Altar Rock is surrounded by other rocks that serve as vivid proof that its name is well deserved.

Visitors to the park are drawn here by the many carvings on the rocks. Time has weathered the scripture verses that were meticulously carved into the sandstone boulders over a hundred years ago, and many are no longer legible. But there are 65 such places spread over the four-and-a-half-acre forested hillside, and easy hiking trails allow the tourist to view them all.

But the focal point of a visit should be the large boulder called Altar Rock. Here, the engraver of the scriptural passages on the other rocks decided to create an open-air chapel where he could conduct worship services for locals drawn to his odd social habits and extreme religious tenets.

Not only did Douglas M. Stahlman hold worship services here, but he built a shelter or cabin against the rock where he made his home for four years. How he managed to provide for himself is not documented,

---

1. Henry W. Shoemaker, "The Story of Altar Rock" *Pennsylvania Mountain Stories*, 13.

Rock # 8 in Scripture Rocks Heritage Park. The inscription thereon reads "Jericho Campaign. July 12 to July 20. Had a vision of a long high wall falling yet will I bring one plague more – the first- born EX.11:1-6 there shall be a great cry Josh. 6:1-20.

Rock # 28 in Scripture Rocks Heritage Park. The inscription here, now barely legible, reads "A rich man shall hard enter into the kingdom of heaven and every one that hath forsaken houses, or brethren or sisters or father, or mother; or wife or children, or lands for my name's sake, shall receive an hundred fold" MAT.19:23-30.

Alter Rock in Scripture Rocks Heritage Park. It was here where the hermit Stahlman built his shelter and where he conducted his outdoor church services.

Still more "Pulpits," located near the intersection of Runk's and Pike Roads on Warrior Ridge between Huntingdon and Alexandria in Huntingdon County, Pulpit Rocks is an amazing collection of stone "pulpits" which are thought by geologists to be some 390 million years old.

The author taking in a grand view of the Lehigh Valley from Pulpit Rock on the Blue Mountain. This Pulpit Rock and view can be found along the Appalachian Trail on the Blue Mountain above the village of Hamburg in Berks County.

but he occupied his time for three years by engraving Biblical passages upon the rocks.

Stahlman had been declared insane while living in Indiana shortly after his wife died from blood poisoning, for which he refused medical help, avowing that prayers and faith alone would be enough to cure her.

He eventually fared no better in Jefferson County, where he returned in 1907; there also declared insane and placed in the county home in 1915. He managed to escape, but after sending threatening letters to county officials, he was recaptured and placed in a mental hospital in Allegheny County, where he died at age 81. His legacy lives on in the form of his rock engravings chiseled into the sandstone boulders at Scripture Rocks Heritage Park, but even that is slowly being erased by the forces of nature, which seemingly care not for Stahlman's hard work nor his sentiments.[2]

---

2. Information found on signs in the park and in the park brochure titled "Scripture Rocks Heritage Park Trail Guide."

LOCATIONS:

Altar Rock can be found on Round Island Ridge in the Bucktail State Park Natural Area of Lycoming County (DD GPS Coordinates: 41.2983965, -77.9936103). From Renovo in Chapman Township of Clinton County, follow Route 120 south past the village of Keating and into Bucktail State Park. The rock is on the ridge across Sinnemahoning Creek, where Round Island Run flows into it.

Scripture Rocks is located in Scripture Rocks Park near Brookville in Jefferson County (DD GPS Coordinates: 41.160530, -79.068801). Follow Route 322 East out of Brookville in Jefferson County and straight onto Route 28 at a Y intersection. Scripture Rocks Park is on the right after one to two miles.

CHAPTER 10

NATIVE AMERICAN MEMENTOES

In addition to the landmarks with Native American associations mentioned in our previous chapters, there are a few lesser-known Native American landmarks that are also worthy of mention in this book. In most cases, they have been largely forgotten or trampled over in humankind's headlong rush toward the future and desire for the benefits of the modern age. Nonetheless, with a little research and dogged persistence, including strenuous hikes along rocky trails and bumpy rides on rough mountain roads, they can be found, and in this chapter, we'll share some of the most intriguing that I have found in my hikes and rough rides through the majestic peaks and lonesome valleys of Pennsylvania.

Many of these spots are little more than place names, leaving us with questions about the origin of the names. One such locale is the spot along Route 45 just outside the small village of Penn Hall in Gregg Township, Centre County. Once known locally as the "Indian Ring," it has been all but forgotten today, and nature has slowly erased most of this once-prominent feature of the hilltop landscape.

According to local sources, this high viewing point was once used by local Indian sentinels to keep watch for intruders while tribal meetings and ceremonies were being held in the nearby clearing. The surveillance spot provided clear views of the entrances to Upper and Lower Penns Valley and nearby Georges and Decker Valleys in the foothills of the Seven Mountains country.

For decades thereafter, clear evidence of the Native American ceremonies at this spot could still be seen in the form of a trench of about thirty-five feet in diameter and ten inches in depth, said to be created by the pounding feet of shouting Indians as they danced around a fire blazing in the center of the ring. Valley settlers became used to the rituals, reporting from time to time that while passing along a nearby northern road, they could sometimes hear the cries of those same Indians.[1]

Today the elements and other natural forces have slowly obliterated the Indian ring, and the mound of charcoal in the center where the ceremonial fires once glowed has eroded too, but careful inspection may yet reveal traces of this once-heralded spot.

The perfect time to do so is, in my opinion, in the fall when leaves of red, gold, and orange flicker and flame on twisted, blackened, and gnarled tree branches. The colorful display is an uncanny reminder of torches glowing in the night, like those carried by Indians who once danced here around their council fires.

Those traveling through Mifflin County along present-day Route 322 pass by yet another forgotten spot which is also said to be associated with the Native Americans who once made this section of the Kishacoquillas Valley their home. The valley's name comes from the most prominent Native American chieftain who lived there. He lived at Ohesson, later called Kishacoquillas' Town, at the mouth of Kishacoquillas Creek, also named after him, and was a firm friend of the first white men who came into his domain.[2]

It is perhaps Shawnee Chief Kishacoquillas who is the "great chief" mentioned in the legend we are about to relate, but as with the case with most legends, the origin of this one, and the historical facts associated with it, are shrouded by the mists of the past.

Bird Rock along the Reedsville Narrows in Brown Township of Mifflin County is not a prominent landmark, but it is more visible now than in the past, thanks to graffiti artists who think their so-called artwork is more important than preserving this unique landmark in its natural state. We've expressed our opinion on such matters in this book, so Bird Rock can

---

1. Dorothy Meyer, "Indian Ceremonial Ring," Chapter XI in a self-published booklet on the legends and tales of Centre County, Pa.
2. C. Hale Sipe, *The Indian Chiefs of Pennsylvania*, 117.

Bird Rock on Jack's Mountain with William G. Jones Jr. (1925–1974). He was a frequent model or subject in photos made by the Kepler Studio, Lewistown. (Photo courtesy of Forest Fisher.)

Bird Rock and tired hikers, from a 1908 colorized postcard. The landmark was a well-known and popular destination for hikers in the early twentieth century, despite the steep and rocky climb required to get there. This view is looking west with the Kishacoquillas Valley in the background. (Photo courtesy of Forest Fisher.)

be added to the list of places destroyed by these self-entitled scoundrels. But despite the desecrations inflicted upon it, Bird Rock's legend seems destined to live on, at least in the pages of this book.

The account of the legend of Bird Rock appeared in a newspaper article and a privately published book some fifty years ago, but where the legend came from was not known at that time, nor has its origin come to light since. Some surmised that it resembles stories once concocted and published by Clinton County folklorist Henry W. Shoemaker, but no evidence has been found to assign its provenance to him. The most likely source of the tale is perhaps the Indians themselves since it is strongly similar to their many accounts of supernatural beings and mystic transformations that stretch the imagination of those of us living in the modern age. See Jesse J. Cornplanter's *Legends of the Longhouse* for several Seneca Indian tales just like this, including "The Legend of the Stone Giants," "The Flying Head," "The Spectre Wife," and others.[3]

The Bird Rock legend we're dealing with begins in the era before white settlers entered the untouched wilderness known today as the Kishacoquillas Valley. The caretakers of this vast wilderness at that period were the sons of the forest, who had lived here for countless centuries, and who were at this time ruled by a "great chief." His name is not preserved in the sad legend associated with the rock that guards the break in Jack's Mountain today, and the mountain's towering cloud-covered peaks may yet hold many similar undiscovered places of legendary lore.

According to the Bird Rock account, the "great chief" had lost his wife when she gave birth to his only child, and it was said he treasured that young daughter "more than life itself" and could refuse her nothing. As she grew older, her devotion to her father grew as well, and she eventually vowed she would never disobey or displease him. Her father tried to ensure that this fidelity would never waver or end by showering his daughter with the finest adornments he could procure, even from places far from his village.

The jewelry undoubtedly included beautiful and elaborately designed earrings, rings, bracelets, and necklaces colorfully decorated with beads of multicolored shells and stones. Pendants of carved wood, animal bones, claws, and teeth could also have been part of her ensemble. But the presents came at a price.

---

3. Jesse J. Cornplanter, "Legends of the Longhouse."

The chief made it clear that as his only child, she could not decide who to marry; it must be his decision; he would choose who her husband must be. At first, the princess accepted this restriction, but as time passed, she realized that she would never marry; her father would never approve of anyone being her husband. This became clear to her as he rejected one suitor after another.

But as often happens, cravings overrule the best intentions, and the passionate Indian princess fell in love with a man she knew her father would never approve of as her husband. Despite her certainty that he would never concede, she tried to persuade her father to accept her choice of a husband, but the chief remained steadfast. Her many tearful entreaties were to no avail, and she finally had to tell her beloved that their cause seemed hopeless.

The young warrior refused to accept defeat, telling his sweetheart they should just run away, that her father would accept him over time and that they could return. But she knew her father would be heartbroken by such a betrayal, and, overcome by anguish and indecision; she ran into the woods and up a mountainside. Her warrior lover ran after her, hoping to stop her mad rush, calm her down, and persuade her to see things his way.

She tried to cut off his pursuit by casting off the precious bracelets, rings, necklaces and a pendant she was wearing, hoping he would be diverted by the valuable objects he could have for the taking. But he had a more precious object he desired, and he continued to chase her to the edge of a mountain cliff. Here, exhausted and forced into what was, in her opinion, a no-win situation, lose her lover or disobey her father, she flung herself over the rim of the precipice and plummeted onto the rocks below.

The exhausted and bereaved warrior could only stand and wail as he looked at the lifeless body of the maiden lying at the base of the cliff. His wails and death shouts were so loud and poignant that the Great Spirit, who had watched the events unfold, was so moved that he immediately decided to change the warrior into a giant stone bird. Thus he could keep a perpetual vigil for his lost love, and it's said he still is there waiting and watching for her to join him once more.[4]

---

4. Benjamin Meyers, "The Legend of Bird Rock," Appeared in the January 8, 1969, issue of the *Lewistown Sentinel*, Lewistown, Pa.

There are more mountain landmarks, or at least place names, that preserve the memory of the last resting places of other Native Americans as well. Indian Grave Run and Indian Grave Road in Fulton County is one such example. Said to be named after an Indian buried near Warfordsburg in that same county, the grave has been lost over time.[5] There is also Indian Hill Road near Boalsburg in Harris Township of Centre County, where, in a nearby field, local historians believe, there was a large Indian burial ground. Evidence of such may be there yet today if archeological studies were conducted.

Similarly, Indian Grave Hill, near Snow Shoe in Centre County, is situated near the site of another Indian village, but there is no longer any evidence to indicate where the last resting places of those Indians might be.

The same might be said of a forgotten cemetery near the small community of Milesburg in that same county. This little country graveyard was once notable for the story of the Native American who is said to be buried there, but it is most remembered today because of its unusual name.

At first, it may seem that Swamp Poodle Cemetery must be a pet cemetery, but the title was coined in Ireland, where it was assigned to marshy areas. Perhaps mistranslated to English, the Irish name became "swamp puddle," which somehow became "swamp poodle" when Irish immigrants brought it to this country after fleeing here from the great potato famine in Ireland in the 1740s.[6]

It would seem then, based on the many McCauslins, McKinleys, and others with similar Irish-sounding names interred in Milesburg's Swamp Poodle Cemetery, that the Irish settlers here felt this name was the most appropriate one for the marshy last resting place of their loved ones.

Local accounts indicate, however, that there is one grave here that is decidedly not that of an Irishman, nor any Englishman at all for that matter. The old story of this gravesite and the large rock that once marked his final resting place tells of someone believed to be the last Indian of the Bald Eagle Valley. He may have been a descendant of one of the inhabitants of the nearby Indian village known as Bald Eagle's Nest. A state historical

---

5. Waterman and Watkins, *History of Bedford, Somerset, and Fulton Counties*, Pa., 666.
6. Ally Schweitzer, "Not just a Silly Name: 'Swampoodle' Park Pays Tribute to D. C.'s Irish Past," American Univ. radio broadcast, December 2017.

A 2021 view of Swamp Poodle Cemetery. Near the village of Milesburg, Centre County, there are no large rocks here that might mark the final resting place of Indian Red.

marker at Milesburg reads: "Bald Eagle's Nest. A Delaware Indian village named for noted Munsee chief Woapalanne or 'Bald Eagle.' Located at union of Spring and Bald Eagle Creeks. From here, raids on the frontier were made in Revolutionary days."

The story of the lone Indian buried nearby comes down to us from Jacob Young, one of the first settlers in the area. Born in 1811, Mr. Young frequently told the story of the Indian's grave to his children and grandchildren, who passed it down to theirs.

Mr. Young often pointed out the Indian's grave beside a large rock in the cemetery, and when doing so, he would tell the story of the man buried there. According to Mr. Young, he was known as "Red Nathan" in his day, and at that time, there once was a large tobacco shed standing along the road leading to the cemetery. In this deserted hovel, recalled Mr. Young, was where Red Nathan lived.

The Indian did not often leave his stark dwelling, but every time he did so, he was belligerent and would provoke a fight with anyone who

The view from Wyalusing Rocks. With the Indian Prayer Rock in the foreground and the horseshoe bend of the Susquehanna River below. To the medicine man who once performed his rituals here, this tranquil and elevated spot must have seemed to be as close to his "Great Spirit" that he would ever get while he was still alive. I had to photoshop my photo to remove all traces of the graffitti disgracefully spray-painted upon the rocks!

happened to be passing by. On one such occasion, his opponent killed him, and residents, glad to be rid of someone they considered a local nuisance, quietly buried him in the unhallowed ground outside the boundary of their oddly-named cemetery. They did not erect a marker over his grave but buried him next to a large boulder, which they decided would be an adequate monument for him.

That large stone cannot be found in the cemetery today, with local logging or road improvements dragging it away or covering it. The cemetery itself is becoming more overgrown and forgotten as the years go by and will gradually disappear if not for maintenance by interested locals.[7]

There is another hallowed landmark, much revered by Native Americans, that seems securely poised to weather the storms of time. Located along historic Route 6 in the picturesque Endless Mountains of Bradford

---

7. Barbara Bruggebors, "Red Nathan Grave Sought," appeared in *The Centre Daily Times*, Bellefonte, Pa., June 4, 1977.

County near Towanda, Wyalusing Rocks overlooks a horseshoe-shaped bend in the Susquehanna River which can be seen in the basin below.

Owned and maintained by the Eastern Delaware Indian Nation, the site holds special significance for Native Americans, who revere it as the high point from which their ancestors could view signals from neighboring tribes and also for being the intersection of two of their most important paths: the Great Warriors Path, which extended from the Hudson River in the north to the Carolinas in the south, and also the Wyalusing Path that led to the important Indian town of Muncy in the southwest. But this place is also regarded by them as having special religious importance.

According to their ancient Susquehannock wise men, "Wyalusing is said to mean 'where there is an old man,' with the 'ng' sound referring to a dwelling." The "old man," they believed, once referred to a holy medicine man who lived and performed devotions at this spot. They, therefore, also referred to the overlook as "Indian Prayer Rock."[8]

More "prayer rocks" at Wyalusing Rocks. These flat outcroppings stick out from the cliff face to the left of the larger prayer rock in the preceding photo. They also would have served as inviting perches for the soothsayer who, legend relates, once performed his rituals here)

---

8. Details found at the following website: http://easterndelawarenations.org/wyrocks.html.

The Flat Rock. Native Americans in present-day Cumberland County may have held this spot in as much reverence as Native Americans esteemed Wyalusing Rocks and its "Prayer Rock" in Bradford County. Those who visit Colonel Denning State Park in Cumberland County are treated to this view at the "Flat Rock" which provides a magnificent view of the Cumberland Valley, and where this rock city is said to have once provided shelter to both mountain lions and Native Americans.

Given the view from this perch, it must have inspired the devoted shaman, especially at sunset when the waters of the river below were shimmering like a pool of mercury and gleaming in the blood-red rays of the setting sun!

Ironically, although Wyalusing Rocks was once a place where the Indians felt closer to their "Great Spirit" and thought he would hear their prayers, their beliefs were sadly shattered by the race that eventually conquered them. As a nearby historical marker indicates, even this holy site and the land around it were not invincible when white frontiersmen overran the area in 1778.

Located about five miles east of Wyalusing Rocks, along Route 6, a state historical sign marks the spot of one of the most decisive battles in Bradford County Indian history. The sign title, "Indian Hill," reads as follows: "The hill just southeast was the scene, September 29, 1778, of a battle between Col. Thomas Hartley's men from Fort Muncy and the Indians. Two days before, Hartley had burned Queen Esther's Town near present-day Athens. Hartley's campaign ended Indian excursions in Bradford County."

It was a sad ending for the Indians, who once regarded this place as one of their most sacred spots.[9]

> LOCATIONS:
>
> **The Indian Ring** is on a hillside near the village of Penn Hall in Centre County (DD GPS Coordinates: 40.86189, -77.55843). The Indian Ring is on private property near the village of Penn Hall, Centre County. No visitors are allowed.
>
> **Bird Rock** stands on top of Jacks Mountain along Mann's Narrows in Mifflin County (DD GPS Coordinates: 40.65472, -77.58351). This is along Route 322 in Mann's Narrows, about two miles west of Lewistown, Mifflin County.
>
> **Swamp Poodle Cemetery** is hidden in shady woods on Dry Top Ridge adjacent to State Game Lands #92 just outside the village of Milesburg, Centre County (DD GPS Coordinates: 40.94173, -77.78500). From Milesburg, follow Moose Run Road over the bridge spanning Bald Eagle Creek. After passing the Route 144 and Route 220 exits, look for an immediate right onto Swamp Poodle Road. Follow this road up to the cemetery.
>
> **Wyalusing Rocks** are preserved in a public park along historic Route 6 in Bradford County (DD GPS Coordinates: 41.69162, -76.27269). The rocks are along historic Route 6 (Grand Army of the Republic Highway) about one mile north of the village of Wyalusing in Bradford County. Look for a small park and pullover on the left. The park is maintained by the Eastern Delaware Nations, but sick graffiti artists have defiled the rocks in their self-entitled disrespectful need to draw attention to themselves. My advice to them is to do something good for the community by getting involved in community service instead of ruining some of the most delightful parts of the community in which you live.

---

9. The Flat Rock: Native Americans in present-day Cumberland County may have held this spot in as much reverence as Native Americans once esteemed Wyalusing Rocks and its "Prayer Rock" in Bradford County. Those who visit Colonel Denning State Park in Cumberland County and hike out to the "Flat Rock" are treated to a magnificent view of the Cumberland Valley and can explore a rock city that is said to have once provided shelter to mountain lions and Native Americans.

CHAPTER 11

THE WITNESS TREE

In our chapter titled "Sentinel Rock," we described a stone pillar regaled in Native American legend as the petrified vault for the spirit of a warrior who failed his tribe miserably when assigned to guard duty. Cursed by his tribe's shaman or medicine man, his spirit was cast into the rock pillar and is destined to spend eternity atoning for his dereliction of duty, to be a silent sentinel forever guarding the pass. But there is another, entirely different, "silent sentinel" that stands along the banks of Penn's Creek, Centre County, and which serves more as a reminder of an event that is said to have occurred here than as an eternal sentry.

The stalwart lone watchman, in this case, is not a stone pillar but a tall dead tree that overlooks the confluence of two creeks and bears witness to a remarkable event that legend and oral history say took place at this spot that locals call "The Forks." As such, it might be better described as a "witness tree" or even possibly a descendant of another tree that once stood here and which may even have been the tree mentioned in the legendary incident over 250 years ago.

Since the supposed event in question occurred so long ago, the tree cited in the old account is unlikely still standing. Extensive lumbering operations probably harvested it along with other giants of the forest that once grew here in the late 1800s, so we will have to settle for the aforementioned "witness tree" as our introduction to the extraordinary event that legend says occurred at this meeting place of the waters.

In the Indian annals of Pennsylvania, there have been many accounts of how Native Americans and white settlers engaged in bloody battles over land ownership. However, as in many historical records of warfare, it is always the victor who "takes the spoils" and has the last word on the conflict, and such is the case with the Indian wars of Pennsylvania. Early historians of that period still were inclined to paint the Native American as a bloodthirsty savage, without regard to how barbaric white settlers could sometimes be in return, and also without regard to how the Native American was mistreated by whites and cheated out of his lands by them. But, as in every war, the more advanced side in science and technology will emerge the victor, and so it was in the Indian wars.

After speaking before a writing class at Lock Haven University one year, I was asked by a brave student why I seemed to be "Indian bashing" in the one book I had written on Pennsylvania mountain folktales and legends, which they had been required to read. I responded that if she were to read all of my books in the series, she would realize I was always coming down on the side of the Indian, giving her the same reasons noted in the previous paragraph. Therefore I include the following tale in this book with the same caveat and with all due respect to Native Americans and their descendants.

One of the most-heralded "Indian fighters" in Penns Valley of Centre County during Pennsylvania's Indian wars was an early settler named Adam Stover. We know little about his exploits other than accounts handed down by word of mouth through the legends and oral history of the area. Those anecdotes indicate that the Indians regarded Stover as a man to be reckoned with. He wore his blond hair longer than most, appearing to be a rough-hewn character, shorn in buckskin clothes and looking like a true frontiersman.

It was also said that he always walked around with a long shiny sword strapped to his side, stopping now and then to take the vicious-looking weapon from its sheath and wave it around in a circle over his head. A flourish intended to intimidate his Indian foes. He was also feared because of his size and strength, exhibiting those traits by sometimes taking hold of both of his grown sons in each hand and easily lifting them off the ground![1]

---

1. Bruce Teeple, Dan Warntz, et. al., *In Schade Vun Rundkopp*, 14-15.

He was also famed far and wide as a man who could not be shot.[2] Whether this was based upon some badly misplaced volleys sent in his direction by his enemies or because he managed to avoid those same bullets in some mysterious way, we will never know, but he no doubt would have encouraged such stories to intimidate his Indian enemies further. And he knew those adversaries well, a font of knowledge which proved to be an advantage on more than one occasion, especially on the night when it is said he rescued a young frontier maiden who Indian warriors had captured.

Residents of the area have handed down this story for almost 250 years.[3] It most certainly struck a chord with those who lived in those times and has also been treasured and preserved by their descendants. It is an account that captures a glimpse into those thrilling decades and adds to the appreciation of their ancestors by those same descendants.

The stirring episode begins during the period of Pennsylvania's Indian Wars known as "the Great Runaway" of 1778. It was a time of fear on the Pennsylvania frontier when Indian war parties, emboldened by their notorious victory at Forty Fort in present-day Luzerne County, descended upon frontier settlements *en masse*, wreaking havoc on farms and cabins. News of the raids spread like wildfire on the frontier, and settlers abandoned their homesteads and sought shelter in the nearest frontier fort.

One of the largest of those forts at that time was Fort Augusta at present-day Sunbury. Built in the 1750s to provide defense during the period known as the French and Indian War, the fortress also served as a haven from Indian attacks during the Revolutionary War. Many such assaults occurred along the West Branch of the Susquehanna in 1778 and 1779, and in a letter dated April 26th, 1779, to Joseph Reed, President of Pennsylvania's Supreme Executive Council (a position equivalent to the governor today), Col. Samuel Hunter, commandant of Fort Augusta at that time, warned: "Our case is really deplorable and alarming, and our county on ye eve of breaking up, as I am informed at the time I am writing this by two or three expresses that there is nothing to be seen but desolation, fire and smoke; as the inhabitants is collected at particular places, the enemy burns all their houses that they have evacuated."[4]

---

2. Ibid.
3. Fred Johnson (born 1942) interviewed by the author on June 10, 2022.
4. C. Hale Sipe, *Indian Wars of Pa.*, 591.

The terror and upheaval spilled over to settlements in the west, and it was then that another Indian event supposedly occurred at that aforementioned place called "the Forks" in Centre County. And not only do the events of that era indicate that such an event could have occurred, but the names preserved in the legendary account correspond to names preserved in the historical record. Moreover, the account itself may reveal an episode that affected Colonel Samuel Hunter, commandant of Fort Augusta, in a very personal way, an incident which seems not to have been preserved in

The witness tree at "The Forks." This swart silent sentinel stands at the same spot where local legend says the young miss Hunter was tied to a tree by Indians. The dead tree in the photo was probably not growing here at that time, but it does serve today as a reminder of the event and also of the local legend regarding her rescue by the heroic Adam Stover.

any accounts of that day, including such comprehensive works as Sipe's *Indian Wars*, Hunter's *Forts on the Pennsylvania Frontier*, or in Samuel Hunter's letters preserved in the *Pennsylvania Archives*.

According to this colorful story, one afternoon at the height of the Indian troubles, the alarm spread quickly among settlements along the banks of the Karoondinha, the Indians' name for the creek, later renamed Penn's Creek by the first settlers, that there was a young woman tied to a tree at "The Forks." Since this was a favorite gathering spot for the Indians, it was quickly realized that she must be a prisoner of those same Indians, and the consensus was that an effort must be made to rescue her.

Many hardy frontiersmen stepped forward to volunteer for the mission, but one of their most respected leaders warned them against it. This holdout was none other than Adam Stover, whose stockaded fortress, known as Stover's Fort (located near present-day Woodward), had provided a welcome refuge from Indian attacks in the past. Stover was respected by his fellows and feared by the Indians and knew more about their mindset and methods than any other man. He was a man to listen to, so the others abandoned their rash plan.

Instead, they agreed with Stover that a more stealthy approach was warranted since some of them were sure to be killed if a battle with the Indians were to occur, and, Stover warned, the young woman would most likely meet the same fate since the Indians would not want to face the humiliation of losing her to any white rescue party. Stover then proposed that he would attempt the rescue by himself, under the cover of darkness.

So it was that on the next moonless night, a log raft or a single large log could be seen floating down the Karoondinha toward "The Forks." By clinging to the log or logs, Adam Stover floated down to the Indian encampment and came ashore near the Indian captive without arousing the sleeping Indians.

Once ashore, he was able to cut the woman's bonds with his knife and then escort her upstream along the Indians' path, described in Paul W. A. Wallace's *Indian Paths of Pennsylvania* as the Karoondinha Path or Penn's Creek Path.[5] From the Forks, the path passed through the present-day

---

5. Paul A. W. Wallace, *Indian Paths of Pa.*, 126.

villages of Millheim, Aaronsburg, and Woodward, and led right to Stover's Fort.

Stover was such an experienced woodsman that he and the exhausted former captive could arrive safely at his fort without even being pursued by the unsuspecting Indians. However, it wasn't long afterward that a party of soldiers from Fort Augusta came to Stover's Fort, inquiring about a young lady the Indians had taken hostage from around Fort Augusta some days earlier.

The young lady, the soldiers related, was an important personage since she was the daughter of Colonel Samuel Hunter, Commandant of Fort Augusta, and he, being much distressed at her capture, had sent them in search of her, naturally supposing the Indians to have traveled west towards their villages. The young lady confirmed that she was indeed the daughter of Colonel Hunter, and it can only be imagined how joyful the reunion between father and daughter must have been when she was brought back safely to Fort Augusta.

Of course, the perfect ending to this story would be that Adam Stover and the young Miss Hunter fell in love, married, and lived happily ever after. However, family genealogists have determined that Adam Stover married Maria Magdalena Troutner in 1776. She bore him a son in 1786, so he was undoubtedly married to her at the time he supposedly rescued Miss Hunter and also during the years after that.[6]

Genealogical information confirms that Colonel Samuel Hunter was the father of two daughters: Mary, "who married Samuel Scott," and Nancy, "who married her cousin Alexander Hunter."[7] Likewise, historical accounts indicate that June and July of 1778 were among the bloodiest times in those horrific days of "The Great Runaway." Those same accounts also indicate that Colonel Hunter decided to send his own family "down the River" along with all the other women and children, fleeing the many Indian attacks and murders occurring daily in the Susquehanna Valley at that time.[8]

One thing we can say with certainty about the women of the Pennsylvania frontier in those days is that they were remarkable for their courage in the face of unbelievable dangers. As noted by one early Pennsylvania

---

6. Found on the web at https://www.wikitree.com/wiki/Stober-12. In Linn's *History of Centre and Clinton Counties* (p. 304), it is noted also that among the first officials of the Salem Evangelical Church in Haines Township in 1794 were Adam Stover and George Troutner (Adam's Father-in-law?).

7. Herbert C. Bell, *History of Northumberland County*, 234.

8. John F. Meginness, *History of Lycoming County*, 140.

historian: "The heroism of the women of the frontier is worthy of the finest strains of the poet's praise. They were worthy of the bravest men that ever shouldered a rifle for the defense of their households. They performed such deeds as belong to the history of the noblest race. In three short years, they were plunged from comfortable homes and prosperous seasons to the depths of desolation and ruin."[9]

Other historical references support that claim, many recalling how young frontier women narrowly escaped attacks by Indian raiding parties. One such account appears in an early history of Wayne Township of Clinton County, where it is noted that during the period of the Great Runaway in 1778, a young lady named Elizabeth Carson, on coming out of a local frontier fort named Fort Horn [Meginness in his *Otzinachson* (p. 216) says this occurred at Antes Fort] "was fired upon by an Indian lying in ambush; the bullet, passing through the folds of her dress, cut fourteen holes in it and left her uninjured!"[10]

But the question remains whether the story about Adam Stover's rescue of the young maiden at "The Forks" is true. To see if there was any historical support for that claim, I looked at the 65 pages containing transcripts of all letters to and from Colonel Hunter preserved in the Pennsylvania Archives Series 1 from 1776 through 1782. In those texts, Colonel Hunter, as Commandant of Fort Augusta, makes many pleas to the Pennsylvania Executive Council for soldiers, muskets, ammunition and funds and asks for orders regarding troop movements. He also includes multiple accounts of Indian attacks to support his pleas for help.

These accounts include many specific details, including dates, exact names, and numbers of settlers, men and women alike, killed, scalped, and taken prisoner by the Indian raiders in those attacks. Colonel Hunter does not mention his daughter being among any prisoners taken in those letters. If such an event had occurred, it would seem that Colonel Hunter would have mentioned it in his letters to the colonial government to add urgency to his requests for help so that he could more readily defend the frontier.

Since Colonel Hunter never indicated that either of his daughters was taken captive by Indians, that alone would indicate that the story of Adam Stover's rescue of Colonel Hunter's daughter may have been nothing more

---
9. Edward MacMinn, *On The Frontier With Colonel Antes*, 357.
10. D. S. Maynard, *Historical View of Clinton County*, 219.

Model of Fort Augusta, located in front of Hunter House at the Northumberland County Historical Society, Sunbury.

than an account designed to glorify Stover.[11] After all, his bravado and daring exploits must have made him seem almost super-human to his compatriots, and so perhaps they wanted to give him credit for this dangerous episode, which could have, after all, actually occurred at "The Forks," but to another young lady rescued by another unsung hero.

Additional Thoughts:

The flight of settlers during the Great Runaway was an unforgettable sight that left a lasting impression on all who saw it. As one West Branch Valley settler later recalled, "I never in my life saw such scenes of distress. The river, and the roads leading down it, were covered with men, women, and children flying for their lives, many without property at all, and none

---

11. Another interesting sidelight about this legend is the fact that the gravestones of both of Colonel Hunter's daughters, Mary and Nancy, can be found near that of their father in the Hunter-Grant pioneer cemetery back of the Northumberland County Historical Society's Hunter House Museum in Sunbury. Evidence that if Native Americans once took either daughter hostage, she was indeed rescued and brought safely back to Fort Augusta.

who had not left the greatest part behind. In short, all of Northumberland County is broken up."[12]

In the same summer of 1778, that chaotic scene was repeated a few miles south of Fort Augusta when a member of the Northumberland County Rangers stationed at Fort Augusta saw a group of refugees fleeing from Penns Valley. He described it as follows: "A flotilla of rafts, canoes and anything else that could float appeared before us here at the fort from the mouth of Penns Creek. The women and boys held muskets and walked on both sides of the creek as a guard."[13]

Although that tireless chronicler of Pennsylvania Mountain stories, Henry W. Shoemaker, included a version of this same tale in a chapter titled "The Lower Fort" among the stories in his *More Allegheny Episodes* (published in 1924), it is an entirely different one than that told to me by valley residents. Shoemaker's is his typical highly romanticized and embellished concoction, but it nonetheless indicates that the story has been around for at least a century, so I included it here in a less embellished form and with some historical background checks.

---

12. Meginness, *op. cit.*, p. 137.
13. Bruce Teeple, *et. al.*, *op. cit.*, 15. The source for this quote is apocryphal. I have not found it in any other historical sources except in the one noted.

CHAPTER 12

LOCHABAR

For anyone who wants to enjoy the glories of nature and, at the same time, feel closer to Pennsylvania's Colonial past, there's probably no better place to start than a historic property located along Antes Creek in Lycoming County. Beautified by a deep blue pool of spring water, which flows down from the heights of Bald Eagle Mountain, the Lochabar estate is a unique area. And its iconic mansion is a quintessential landmark, a surprising survivor of the past and an amazing link to another age.

As far as can be determined, the large stone mansion dates back to 1769, when hardy Scotchman Ralph Forster laid its cornerstone. It served as his residence and as a refuge for Forster and his neighbors when many sanguinary battles occurred between the settlers and unfriendly Native Americans. At that time, it became known as "Forster's Fort" until the Indian troubles subsided, after which time a mill was erected near here, and the site became the prosperous village of Mill Port.

No evidence of the village of Mill Port exists today, the village having been swept completely away in the great flood of 1889, and the current name of the locale, "Lochabar," meaning "Lake of Horns," is no doubt of Scottish origin since a lake of that name still exists in that country. However, it seems more likely that canny Scot Ralph Forster did not refer to it that way but that the more recent owner and historian George L. Sanderson designated it as such.

On the other hand, the name of the deep blue pool of mountain spring water near the mansion house seems to have also changed over the years.

Today it's known as "Wiidagh's Spring since an Indian chief of that name is suspected of having made his village here (see the chapter titled "King Wiidagh's Grave" in this volume for details and for a ghost tale that was once told about the spring). But many at the turn of the nineteenth century were said to sometimes refer to it as the "Widow's Spring," owing to ownership at that time by two widows.[1] Yet others, it is thought, were inclined to call it the "Enchanted Spring," perhaps because of its unnatural deep blue color and due to its weird, yet beautiful, surroundings—stately pines and hemlocks whose dense canopy still darkens the nearby forest even on the brightest days.[2]

But a curious discovery in a walled-up section of the basement of the old manor house in 1876 cast an even darker shadow upon the estate, giving it an unwelcome notoriety. When George Sanderson decided to remodel his ancient pile in 1876, he resolved to tear down the basement wall that appeared to conceal a hidden room. However, what he discovered inside formed the basis for an enduring marvelous narrative and a gruesome mystery that remains unsolved today.

Sanderson was not prepared for what he found lying inside the secret compartment. There, grinning up at him, was a human skull lying beside a heap of bones covered by what appeared to be a military uniform of an earlier day. Upon closer inspection, Sanderson, in the dim light, could also discern a long sword that appeared to be of British military origins. A mess kit and other utensils were also in the fifteen by-twenty-foot room.

The grisly remains did not easily cow Sanderson, and, being an avid historian, his curiosity was stimulated. He, therefore, subsequently sent the buttons on the uniform to England for verification. There it was confirmed that the buttons were from the Revolutionary War period and were authentic. Likewise, the sword was identified as being identical to one carried by Hessian soldiers in that same war. Subsequent forensic examination determined that the bones were of a young man who was approximately 23 years old when he died.

Was the soldier imprisoned in that unholy tomb by local patriots who, during the Revolutionary War years or in the years immediately thereafter,

---

1. Wayne O. Welshans, "A Nippenose Collection," Section titled "The Widow's Spring."
2. Ibid., Section titled "The Enchanted Spring."

held a vengeful grudge against the troops they had fought against? They held special disdain for the Hessians, German mercenaries hired by the British to fight the English colonists, and perhaps this one had deserted from his unit and, in his flight, had been apprehended by his enemies, who gave him no quarter.

Then too, perhaps in the unforgiving subzero winds of a harsh Central Pennsylvania winter, the unfortunate soldier had gotten lost, became separated from his unit, and sought shelter in the root cellar of the old fort. There, unable to keep warm, he may have frozen to death. That scenario, of course, does not consider why his last resting place was walled up, seemingly to ensure he would never be found. It is an account that seems like it could have only been written by Edgar Alan Poe, that master of horror whose tale titled "The Cask of Amontillado" has elements that are eerily similar to the fate that seems to have befallen the unfortunate soldier whose life ended at Lochabar.

The Sandersons[3] preserved the skull (now lost) and sword found in their "dungeon," placing the skull on their fireplace mantle with the sword hanging over that same fireplace in the living room of the manor house, both serving as reminders of the estate's colorful past. But an even more remarkable artifact, also once preserved in Lochabar's archives, is a silver medal discovered in the nineteenth century near Aughanbaugh's Gap on Bald Eagle Mountain.

It is only three inches in diameter but was made to endure, with a silver content of six ounces. Upon one side is engraved a relief profile of President James Madison, and on the other, the words "Peace and Friendship" with

---

3. The Sanderson family were direct descendants of one Robert Covenhoven, who is regaled in the histories of the West Branch Valley as a fearless scout and Indian fighter during the Revolutionary War. His many exploits can be found in *The History of the West Branch Valley* by Meginness, in Sipe's *Indian Wars of Pennsylvania*, and many others. His courage and survival skills are almost unparalleled compared to other brave frontiersmen of that day. Remarkably, the Sandersons preserved a portrait of this larger-than-life personage and some of his personal frontier artifacts. All can be found today at the Taber Museum in Williamsport. Some doubt has arisen that the portrait is of Covenhoven, but authentication of it appeared in an article in the September 6, 1916, *Williamsport Gazette and Bulletin* written by local historian Colonel Thomas Lloyd, who states, "Years ago, an excellent oil painting of the famous pioneer (Covenhoven) adorned the walls of Lochabar, and there were many relics of interest too."

an image of the clasped hands of what appears to be a colonial officer and an Indian, above which is an image of a crossed tomahawk and peace pipe.[4]

Some once conjectured that the medal was presented as a token of friendship by colonial authorities to either Chief Nippenuce, for whom the valley is named, or to Chief Wiidagh, whose village once stood at Lochabar. However, Madison's picture on the medallion renders that belief untenable since Madison's term of office was from 1809 to 1817, while Wiidagh and Nippenuce lived during the colonial era a hundred years earlier.

So it would seem that the reason the silver medallion was cast and for whom it was intended will most likely remain as great a mystery as why the Hessian soldier's remains were walled up the way they were. An even greater mystery is why the medallion ended up on the mountain. Perhaps it had been cast aside by a descendant of one of the chiefs, who had inherited it as it was passed down through the generations.

As years went by and the wrongful ways the white man had claimed Native American lands became more evident, the medallion's owner perhaps could not look upon it as a relic of distinction but rather as an objectionable reminder of past wrongs done to his race.[5]

The silver medallion on display at the Taber Museum in Williamsport. Once part of the Lochabar archives, it was donated to the museum by Mrs. Emily Sanderson Carter.

Back of the silver medallion. I'm indebted to the staff of the Taber Museum for opening their display cases so I could get good photos of the Lochabar artifacts.

---

4. W. H. Sanderson, "Reminiscences of W. H Sanderson; Robert Covenhoven, The Famous Scout," *Journal of the Lycoming County Historical Society*, Volume V, No. 1 Spring 1968, p. 12.

5. Ibid., Section titled "Lochabar and its surroundings."

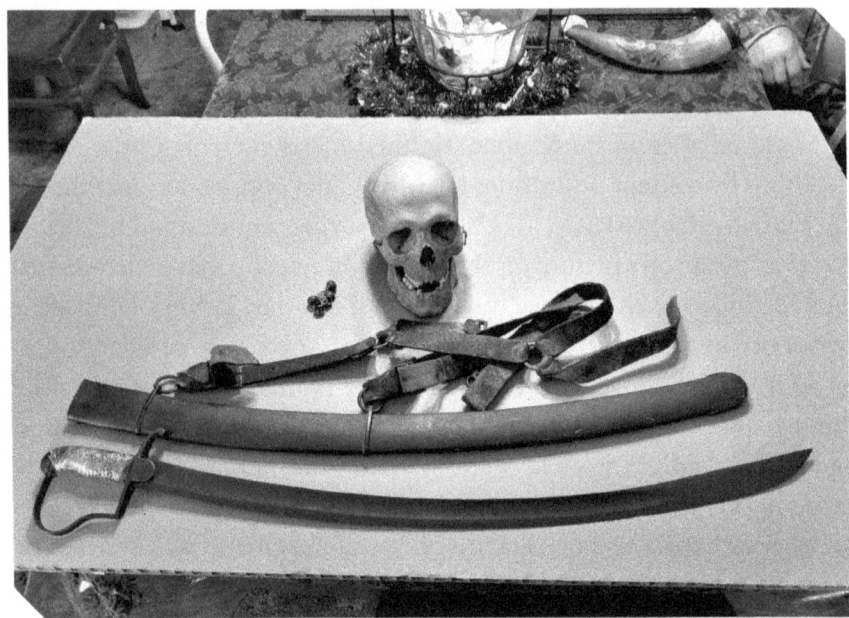

The skull and the sword. An earlier family photo of the items found in the Lochabar "dungeon" by the Sanderson family in 1876, one hundred years after the man entombed there breathed his last breath. The photo shows the man's skull, buttons off of his uniform jacket, and his sword and scabbard. The skull has been lost over the years, but the family still has the other artifacts.

The Lochabar "dungeon" as it appears today. Photo of the entrance knocked out by the Sandersons.

The Lochabar "dungeon" as it appears today. Photo of the interior showing the stone slab upon which the skeleton was found.

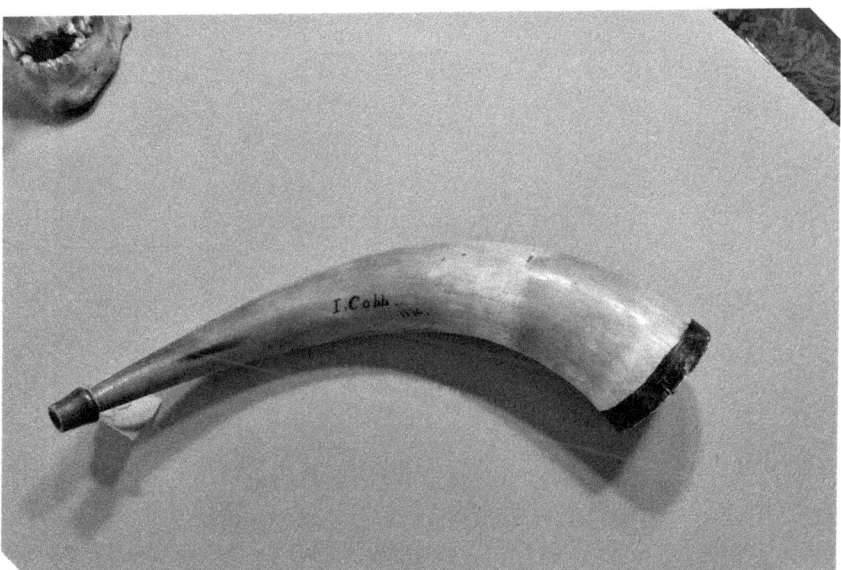

The Powder Horn. In addition to the other artifacts found in the Lochabar "dungeon," there was also a powder horn that was said to have a man and woman's likeness etched upon it, along with a notation of "N. Morgan, 1776". The powder horn, like the skull, has been lost over time. The one shown in the photo is a modern-day replicate, preserved at the manor house. It was created for decorative purposes and so is of much later origin than indicated by its notation of "I. Cobb, 1776". One has to wonder if N. Morgan was the name of the Hessian soldier who died in the dungeon. DNA tests might be able to provide some clues today, if the skull could be found!

Lochabar Manor House. Still a picturesque setting today, with the Bald Eagle Mountain in the background and the stone pillars astride the driveway entrance. This is private property and should be respected as such.

Portrait of Robert Covenhoven on display at the Taber Museum in Williamsport. Once part of the Lochabar archives, it was also donated to the museum by Mrs. Emily Sanderson Carter. W. H. Sanderson, born in 1837, was his great grandson. He knew Covenhoven personally and listened attentively at his knee as this 90-year-old former frontier scout told him many tales of the frontier and of the Revolutionary War, having crossed the Delaware with George Washington and fighting alongside him at the Battle of Trenton. Sanderson's description of his great grandfather is an amazing pen picture of this remarkable Pennsylvania frontiersman (see footnote 4).

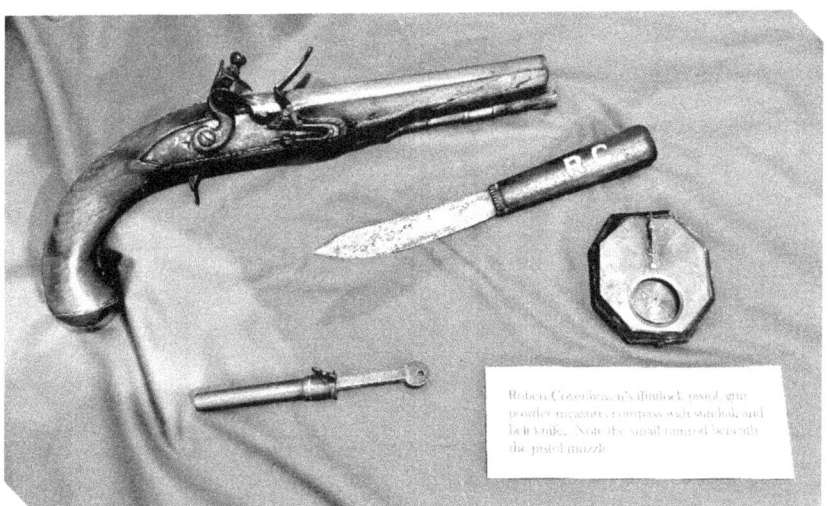

Robert Covenhoven's Frontier Accessories on display at the Taber Museum in Williamsport. Also once part of the Lochabar archives, they were donated to the museum by Mrs. Emily Sanderson Carter. The artifacts include Covenhoven's flintlock pistol with ramrod, gun powder measure, compass with sundial, and a knife adorned with his initials. He is said to have prized the knife very highly along with his hunting knife, which was filed with twelve or thirteen notches on the back of its long black handle – one for each Indian whose life he had taken in his many struggles on the frontier.

CHAPTER 13

A TIMELY REMINDER

One of the most comprehensive and trusted histories of the West Branch Valley of east-central Pennsylvania is the work *Otzinachson, or A History of the West Branch Valley of the Susquehanna*, by John F Meginness. He was a tireless and meticulous chronicler of the events and people that created the colorful historic tapestry of this scenic locale, and he did so when many of those whose memories extended back to the earliest days of the valley were still alive to tell about it.

For instance, Meginness' *Otzinachson* was published in 1857, and one of his contemporaries at that time was Anna Jackson Hamilton, who died five years later at age 94. It was said that her mind and memory were "keen to the end," that Meginness "often visited her," and that he acknowledged "his debt to her for many of the tales he related."[1]

Mrs. Hamilton, having been born in 1768, was just ten years old at the time when one of the terrifying episodes of the West Branch Valley sent settlers fleeing from their homes to seek shelter in the nearest frontier forts, a time historians now refer to as "The Big Runaway," or "The Great Runaway."

Instigated by an Indian uprising perpetrated by British troops during the Revolutionary War, the events that unfolded caused widespread destruction and death upon what was then considered the Pennsylvania frontier. So many settlers fled their homes and farms that the sight was indelibly

---

1. Helen Herritt Russell, "The Great Runaway of 1778," *Proceedings of the Northumberland County Historical Society*, Volume 23, 1960, p. 1.

printed upon the young mind of Mrs. Hamilton, who had witnessed the panicky "fleeters," as they were called, firsthand.

"You couldn't possibly count the people—might as well try to count the raindrops in a cloud!" was the way she tried to recall it when asked about it in her later years.[2]

Meginness no doubt had other people whom he considered to be reliable sources for tales of the previous century, and one such person was John Foster, Esq., of Buffalo Crossroads, who, Meginness noted, "remembers many incidents of Indian history and many more interesting reminiscences of Buffalo Valley."[3] He then goes on to relate one of Foster's more interesting tales, which was as follows: "One night, his family was alarmed by Indians and fled to a rye patch adjoining the house, where they passed the night. A small dog, that was usually very vociferous at night, stayed with them and made *no* noise." The family always considered it a special act of Providence. Next morning plenty of Indian tracks were found around the house. It was a log building and is standing at the present day."[4]

And your author has visited that historic structure, which, as of 2019, was still standing, yet, serving as a remarkable corroboration as to the veracity of Foster's account! I had not known of his recollection in Meginness' *Otzinachson* at the time I was writing about a similar episode I had just been told about that was said to have occurred near Buffalo Crossroads in Buffalo Valley of Union County (see my *Pennsylvania Fireside Tales Volume VII* for a chapter recounting the story). Now I consider Foster's recollection to be validation of one of the most remarkable events I have yet collected in my endeavor to preserve the mountain folktales and legends of Pennsylvania, even though the family name in the story told to me was Sierer, not Foster.

Nonetheless, the similarities between the Foster and Sierer tales are so extraordinary that I'm sure Foster was mistaken about the family name. And there is an astonishing local landmark that seems to confirm this conclusion.

---

2. Ibid.
3. John F. Meginness, *Otzinachson*, 408.
4. Ibid.

Sitting "off the beaten path" at the end of a long country lane beside Beaver Run in Buffalo Township of Union County and near the quaintly-named village of Buffalo Crossroads, there is an ancient stone farmhouse, built over 200 years ago, that evokes a nostalgic feeling in those who pass by the old place. Perhaps it is the size of the trees that stand in the front yard that provide a clue as to the age of the homestead, or maybe it's just the old-time architecture that conveys the same message, but whatever the case, it is a delight to behold, particularly when a closer look is taken at the east face of the house, and the eyes wander up to the rooftop.

Here, located just under the roof peak, are two stones different from the other field stones used to build the manor house. On both these stones, some inscriptions and engravings turned the monoliths into memorials of another, more deadly, time. The lowest block is rectangular and is engraved with the letters "J H S 1795 S N S," which, according to the present owner of the picturesque farm, records the year the house was built and the initials of the husband and wife who built it: Johannes and Susannah Sierer. But above the rectangular stone is a square one with a more ambiguous engraving upon it, an engraving assured to mystify and intrigue anyone who sees it.

The date on the square block, 1795, also commemorates the date the place was built, but below that date is a clock face, complete with Roman numerals, and an hour and a minute hand set at exactly 11:45. Fortunately, the reason the odd decoration was added to the date stone has been faithfully preserved by the farm's string of owners over the years. When a new farm owner takes it over, he is also given two other things.

First, he is handed the original deed to the farm conveyed to Edward and Joseph Shippen by Thomas and John Penn, sons of William Penn, in 1705. The legal language inked upon the thick parchment in flowery black lettering is amazing to behold and only adds to the value of this remarkable artifact, which the farm's owners always cherish. But the second thing buyers are given when they purchase the farm, the story of the clock face, is something the new owners appreciate almost as much as the original deed since both date back to colonial times.

The story of the clock face was told to us one cold winter day in 2019 when the friendly farmer who currently owns the place took time from

A TIMELY REMINDER

The ancient parchment, deed from the sons of William Penn to the Shippens.

The clockface with its bequiling message.

The Sierer's original log cabin. Much enlarged and modernized, its original fireplace and one of its original log walls can still be seen inside today. The field where the Sierer's hid in the flax can also still be seen on the hillside back of the cabin.

his barn chores to pause and take our minds back again to the time of the Great Runaway. In addition to showing us the aforementioned deed, the young man also recalled the event that led to engraving the clock face on the stone under the east roof peak of the Sierer's mansion.

According to our storyteller, the Sierers didn't originally live here. At the time of the Great Runaway in 1778, the family residence was an old log cabin just a short distance south of the present house. It was here one night in 1778 that the Sierer's dog began barking and fussing enough that the Sierers became alarmed. Looking outside, they could, with sufficient moonlight, discern, across one of their fields and, at some distance, a band of Indians trying to sneak up on the unsuspecting family.

The dog's timely warning gave the settlers just enough time to make a stealthy exit out the back of the cabin and hide in a rye field behind the cabin. Upon finding the homestead empty, the Indians vented their frustrations by ransacking the place, which apparently tired them so much

A view of the field in back of the Sierer log cabin where they hid in the flax that was growing here at the time of the Indian raid.

that they left without making sufficient effort to determine whether any of the cabin's former inhabitants were still in the area.

The Sierers must have felt God himself had intervened on their behalf that night, and that was something they didn't want to forget. To ensure they did not, they decided to engrave a clock face on the date stone of their new house. The time they decided to put on that face was 11:45—the precise moment their dog had warned them of the Indian marauders that were coming to kill them and carry away their scalps.[5]

---

5. The field where the rye was planted and where the Sierers hid from the Indians can still be seen behind the original Sierer log cabin, which, although covered in aluminum siding and modernized in other ways, still contains one of the cabin's original log walls and its original stone fireplace. The clockface on the Sierer's grand stone manor house is also an extraordinary landmark and a tangible link to Pennsylvania's colonial past. In addition to the current owners of the Sierer's stone manor house and farm, I'm also indebted to the current owners of the Sierer's original log cabin, who so graciously invited me inside to take pictures of the original log wall and fireplace and who confirmed details of the Sierer's story.

CHAPTER 14

BEARTOWN ROCKS

Among the fabulous "rock cities" in Centre County is one that has, for all practical purposes, been largely forgotten. Located on Bear Knob north of the small community of Unionville in Union Township and along the thoroughfare locals still refer to as the Rattlesnake Pike in Moshannon State Forest, it is somewhat hidden. But it also conceals a large cave where bears once made their winter dens and still may do so, probably because they like the privacy it affords. But when bears forsake the cave for lush forest dens come warmer weather, it is sometimes taken over by hunters who use it for shelter when cooking their meals while on hunting trips, as evidenced by the soot-blackened ceiling of the cave entrance.[1]

Although those same hunters may not have thought about it, the rock city no doubt takes its name from the black bears that have, for centuries, found the cave an ideal sheltering place come winter. For a time, however, another popular story claimed the name was "Baretown" Rocks, not "Beartown" Rocks at all, and that there was an Indian legend that explained its origins.

This so-called Indian legend, however, is so fantastic and improbable that its source has to be suspect. And, not surprisingly, it came from the facile pen of one Henry W. Shoemaker, that early collector of central Pennsylvania legends and folktales, who, as noted in Chapter 6, is well-known for his embellishments and fabrications.

Shoemaker's story, "The Antiquity of Baretown," appears in his volume of folktales titled *Pennsylvania Mountain Stories* (Altoona Press 1911). In

---

1. Paul M. Dubbs, *Where to Go, & Place-Names of Centre County*, 141.

A rock bridge at Beartown Rocks in Clear Creek State Park.

that essay, Shoemaker refers to the rocks as Baretown instead of Beartown, either because he was unaware of the true spelling or because he wanted to rename the rocks to align with the story he concocted. And that narrative is typical of Shoemaker's penchant for lurid and romanticized accounts of Pennsylvania's Native Americans.

In his chronicle, Shoemaker tells of an ancient white race who lived in the mountains here tens of thousands of years ago and were so powerful that they were able to enslave their Native American neighbors and force them to build a huge stone palace at the place now called Beartown. The palace, says Shoemaker, was built to satisfy the whims of the ruler of the master race, who wanted it built to win the heart of a beautiful maiden of one of his "subjects."

However, after years of hard labor in quarrying, transporting, and fitting huge rocks together to build a palace for the cruel ruler of their white masters, the Indians finally had enough. On the day the palace was to be dedicated, several concealed themselves behind the towering rock walls,

One of the rock city pathways between huge boulders at Beartown Rocks in Clear Creek State Park.

which were held tenuously in place by wooden derricks until they could be more permanently secured.

Then, while the white race was engrossed in the dedication ceremonies, some of the Indian saboteurs began sawing through the wooden supports until the walls tumbled down upon their white masters, killing them all and leaving the jumble of huge rocks that can be seen yet today at Shoemaker's "Baretown."

Later generations, intrigued by Shoemaker's claims, decided to subject them to the sharp lens of scientific inquiry. An organization was therefore commissioned to investigate the site, and the New England Antiquities Research Association (NEARA), after a thorough investigation, concluded that Baretown Rocks "bore no signs of human construction or activity" and was merely a product of normal glacial and climactic upheavals.[2] A conclusion that seems entirely plausible when compared to Shoemaker's claims that the room-sized boulders here could have been used to build a palace for his imagined "king."

---

2. Barbara Bruggebors, "Boulders are Beartown's Big Claim to Fame," *Centre Daily Times* of State College, September 22, 1984.

The viewing platform on the large rock at Beartown Rocks in Clear Creek State Park.

Shoemaker's inspirations for his Pennsylvania legends often came from European legends, but in this case, however, he also might have had an inspiration from the Holy Bible, where in Joshua 10:11, it is written that "As the Amorites retreated down the road from Beth-horon, the Lord destroyed them with a terrible hailstorm from heaven that continued until they reached Azekah. The hail killed more of the enemy than the Israelites killed with the sword."

There is yet another Beartown in Pennsylvania that has not been subjected to Shoemaker's hyperbole, even though geologists describe it as one of the largest rock outcroppings in the state.

Located in northern Jefferson County's Clear Creek State Forest, the name Beartown would suggest it is named that way because bears once favored it for their dens, just like those of Beartown in Centre County. However, when I asked one of Clear Creek State Park's current park rangers if she knew why the rocks received that name, she said she did not, nor did she know of any legends about it.

The magnificent view of the Clarion River system from the viewing platform at Clear Creek State Park.

However, I am certain that the many rock crevices and cave-like openings here would serve, and did serve, as ideal dens for bears, and that fact, coupled with the way the pathways through the huge boulders here resemble the streets of a small town, convinces me that the name Beartown was chosen for those reasons.

Although the Park ranger at Clear Creek did not know why her Beartown rocks got that name, she informed me of another rock in the park with an interesting story. Irish Rock, along the Irish Rock Trail beside the Clarion River, got that name, says the ranger, either because it's shaped like Ireland or because loggers floating logs down the Clarion River could leave money for and pick up jugs of Irish Whisky left there by local moonshiners.

But the rocks at Clear Creek's Beartown draw curious sightseers and nature lovers. They come here to hike the Beartown Rocks Trail and see the house-sized boulders, up to 20 feet tall, scattered throughout the woods. They also are attracted by the beautiful views of the Clarion River Valley that can be seen from atop a wooden viewing platform perched on a massive stone outcropping. It is well worth the effort to climb the viewing

Another rocky pathway beside towering rocks and overhangs at Beartown Rocks in Clear Creek State Park.

tower's steps to get a bird's eye view of one of America's Wild and Scenic river systems.

The huge rocks here at Clear Creek's Beartown were, just like those in Centre County's Beartown, deposited and rearranged by glaciers over 22,000 years ago. The only differences between the two, therefore, would seem to be that Centre County's Beartown is on private property and not open to the public, while Clear Creek's rocks are publicly accessible and are also unsullied by Henry Shoemaker's fabrications.

LOCATIONS: Beartown Rocks in Centre County is located in Moshannon State Forest on Bear Knob, northwest of Unionville. Beartown Rocks in Jefferson County are located in Clear Creek State Park (DD GPS Coordinates: 41.30137, -79.05823). Beartown Rocks in Centre County are on private property. To get to Jefferson County's Beartown Rocks, go to Clear Creek State Park and Turn off Corbett Road at the Beartown Rocks sign. Proceed to the parking area just a few hundred yards ahead.

CHAPTER 15

THE ROCK GARDEN

In their interesting local history titled "Pioneering With Sullivan County Pioneers," authors Pauline Holcombe and Mildred Lundy recall what the first settlers in this unsettled wilderness had to endure to survive. They also describe the intimidating environment the settlers encountered, especially in the forests of what is now World's End State Park.

"The discovery of this 'Sylvan Eden' is shrouded in mystery," the authors begin, saying it was then part of "a vast unexplored wilderness for perhaps two hundred years."[1]

As such, the land ownership was disputed for decades, with Native Americans having the "right of discovery" since they had established temporary campsites here long before the white settlers began to make inroads to this sylvan paradise. The subsequent discovery of arrowheads, spearheads, flint knife blades and other relics at these places support these contentions, but as in similarly contested lands in Pennsylvania, it was the white man who always gained the upper hand, especially as the Indians were gradually decimated by smallpox and famine.

Even after wresting the land from the Indians, those same early white settlers still had many hardships to endure, including finding enough food to survive. Their constant battle to grow crops, kill wild game, and harvest roots and berries in the wild was made difficult by the primeval forest

---

1. Pauline Holcombe and Mildred Lundy, *Pioneering with Sullivan County Pioneers*, Endicott Publishing Company, Endicott, NY, 1953.

surrounding them. As one early historian described the area at that time, "No roads, few streams navigable for canoes, small streams choked with fallen timber and underbrush, narrow valleys filled with thickets of hemlock and laurel, deep gorges, swamps and high mountains combined to impede their progress."[2]

Over a hundred years later, some 20 years after Daniel Ogdens became the first settler here in 1786,[3] the ability to navigate through the area was not much better, even though there was now a narrow roadway, built in 1810, that penetrated the once-impenetrable wilderness.

"It is grand and picturesque beyond description," one early traveler described the trip. "Here hills peep o'er hills and Alps o'er Alps arise. The road passing the Worlds End is on the south side and, strange as it may seem, is constructed on the narrow gauge principle, without a single turn-out for passing vehicles. Three hundred feet below, nearly perpendicular, bubbles and boils the sable waters of the Loyalsock. On the other side are steep banks of earth or solid rock. Happy is he who runs this gauntlet without encountering a traveler going in the opposite direction!"[4]

Today this picturesque corner of the Allegheny Highlands Plateau, known as the Sullivan Highlands, remains part of the Endless Mountains of Pennsylvania. Moreover, due to the efforts of the boys of the Civilian Conservation Corps in the 1930s, it has been designated by Pennsylvania's Department of Conservation and Natural Resources (see their website) as "one of Twenty Must-See Pennsylvania State Parks." Describing it as "virtually in a class by itself" they note that "this wild, rugged, and rustic area seems almost untamed."

Such description no doubt draws visitors to World's End to experience its isolation and natural environment, but they may also sometimes be drawn here solely based on its name. The designation conveys an impression that this place is like that of the proverbial "back of the Great Beyond" sought by adventurers. However, although it is almost a wilderness in some places today, there is still some uncertainty about why it was named the way it was.

---

2. Ibid.
3. Ibid.
4. *THE VISTA, Newsletter of the Friends of World's End State Park* Volume 4, No. 1, Winter 2022.

Some say the name was originally "Whirl's End", which was a combination of the words "Worlds End" and "whirlpool." That conjecture is based on the existence of a turbulent whirlpool that was once one of the most unusual features of Loyalsock Creek. Although the whirlpool is no longer there, the creek still courses through this rugged wilderness. Others say that the name "Worlds End" is the better title since it came from the opinions of the first travelers who journeyed into this inhospitable and impassable wilderness and thought they had reached "the end of the world!" Whatever the case may be, the Worlds End label won out after the whirlpool disappeared, and it does seem the more appropriate of the two options, given the landscape that is still here today.[5]

Sullivan County is home to World's End State Park and part of Ricketts Glen State Park, famous for its numerous waterfalls. But it's the many mountain vistas that visitors to this part of the state can enjoy, and Worlds End boasts a notable overlook of its own. The view requires a hike up the park's Canyon Vista Trail, but the effort will reward trekkers with a spectacular panorama of the Loyalsock Creek Gorge and other parts of the area known locally as the Sullivan Highlands.

But the park and its surroundings also have other noteworthy attractions, including a lake to the south with a haunted reputation. However, to learn more about the story of Eaglesmere Lake and the origins of its ghost tale, readers are directed to the author's Pennsylvania Fireside Ghost Tales (see the chapter titled "Misty Moonbeams and Foggy Nights").

Within World's End State Park itself, other landmarks attract those drawn to the rare and unusual, including an assembly of monumental boulders that are another of the park's natural wonders. Access to The Rock Garden, as it's styled, is another plus for those who hike up the Canyon Vista Trail to the grand overlook. The gigantic rocks in the "garden" form a baffling and impressive maze that provides an interesting diversion for those who want to explore wild and mysterious places. But there is a similar spot just east of the park that rock lovers will also appreciate.

The Haystacks, as they're called, can be found protruding from the waters of Loyalsock Creek along Route 220 just north of Laporte. The view of these rocky natural wonders requires hiking up some moderately rugged

---

5. *Recreational Guide for World's End State Park,* Publication of Pennsylvania Department of Conservation and Natural Resources.

The Haystacks and Dutchman's Falls in Loyalsock Creek at World's End State Park

trails to reach them, but once there, the hiker can see that they resemble small old-fashioned haystacks, the kind Little Boy Blue of nursery rhyme fame fell asleep under. A view of Dutchman's Falls at this same spot is yet another reward for those who make the trek back here, but if it's ghosts you're after, then you need to return to Worlds End State Park and then head south to the aforementioned Lewis' Lake at nearby Eagles Mere.

Once there, walk along the narrow Laurel Path, as locals call it, and through areas overgrown with almost impenetrable Rhododendron stands, creating dark tunnels along this lakeside glen. This trail leads to the infamous "Lover's Rock," the site of the aforementioned ghost tale.

LOCATION: **World's End State Park** is located in the Loyalsock Creek Valley south of Forksville, Sullivan County (DD GPS Coordinates: 41.4718, -76.58145). The park is along PA 154 and is easily reached from PA 87 from Williamsport and west; PA 42 from I-80 and south; and PA 87 from Dushore and the north and east.

Loyalsock Canyon Vista at World's End State Park.

My late wife standing in the Rock Garden at World's End State Park.

THE ROCK GARDEN

Lost among the rocks! One of the many stacks of boulders in the Rock Garden at World's End State Park.

A narrow passageway between the boulders in the Rock Garden at World's End State Park.

Another view of large boulders in the Rock Garden at World's End State Park.

BIBLIOGRAPHY

Africa, J. Simpson, *History of Huntingdon and Blair Counties Pennsylvania*, Louis H. Everts, Philadelphia, 1883.
Baughman, Ernest W., *Type and Motif Index of the Folktales of England and North America—Indiana University Folklore Series #20*, Mouton and Co., The Hague, Netherlands, 1966.
Beers & Company, *Historical and Biographical Annals of Columbia and Mountour Counties, Pa. (Volume I)*, J. H. Beers & Co., Chicago, 1915.
Bell, Herbert C., *History of Northumberland County*, Brown, Runk, & Co., Chicago, 1891.
Craft, The Reverend David; *1770-1878 History of Bradford County, Pennsylvania, with Illustrations and Biographical Sketches of Some of its Prominent Men and Pioneers*, L. H. Everts & Co., Philadelphia, Pa., 1878.
Cummings, Uriah, *Song of U-RI-ON-TAH*, Courier Co., Buffalo, N. Y., 1900.
Day, Sherman, *Historical Collections of the State of Pa.*, Ira J. Friedman, Port Washington, N. Y., 1843.
Donehoo, George P., *Indian Villages and Place Names in Pennsylvania*, Telegraph Press, Harrisburg, Pa., 1928.
Dubbs, Paul M., *Where to Go and Place-Names of Centre County*, Centre Daily Times, State College, Pa., June 1961.
Freeze, John Gosse, *A History of Columbia County, Pa.*, Elwell & Bittenbender, Publisher, Bloomsburg, Pa., 1883.
Grimm, Jacob, *Teutonic Mythology*, George Bell & Sons, London, 1882.
Heckewelder, Rev. John, *History, Manner, & Customs of the Indian Nations*, Lippincott's Press, Philadelphia, 1876.
Holcombe, Pauline and Lundy, Mildred, *Pioneering With Sullivan County Pioneers*, Endicott Publishing Company, Endicott, NY, 1953.
Imhof, John D., *Elk County—A Journey Through Time, Volume One*, Baumgratz Publishing, St. Marys, Pa. 2019.
Linn, John Blair, *History of Centre and Clinton Counties, Pennsylvania*, Louis H. Everts Co., Philadelphia, 1883.

Lyman, Robert R., Forbidden Land: *Strange Events in the Black Forest*, The Potter Enterprise, Coudersport, Pa., 1971.
Lytle, Milton Scott, *History of Huntingdon County in the State of Pennsylvania*, Milton S. Roy, publisher, Philadelphia, 1876.
MacMinn, Edward, *On the Frontier With Colonel Antes*, S. Chew & Sons, Camden, N. J., 1900.
Maynard, D. S., *Historical View of Clinton County*, Enterprise Printing House, Lock Haven, Pa. 1875.
McCool, Sarah Ann, "Historical Gleanings of Schuylkill County Pa. (Chapter XLI)," originally published by Thomas J. Foster in the *Shenandoah Weekly Herald*, Shenandoah, Pa., from Feb. 7, 1874 to Nov. 27, 1875.
Meginness, John F., *History of Lycoming County Pa.*, Brown, Runk & Co., Chicago, 1892.
———, *Otzinachson, A History of the West Branch Valley*, Gazette Printing House, Williamsport, Pa, 1889.
Rung, Albert M., *Rung's Chronicles of PA History*, Huntingdon County Historical Society, Huntingdon, Pa., 1984.
Shoemaker, Henry W., *Eldorado Found*, Altoona Tribune Publishing, Altoona, Pa., 1917.
———, *Pennsylvania Mountain Stories*, Reading Times Publishing Co., Reading, Pa., 1911.
———, *Tales of the Bald Eagle Mountains*, Bright Printing Company, Reading, Pa., 1912.
Sinclair, Sir John of Ulster, *The Statistical Account of Scotland, Volume 8*, W. Creech, Edinburgh Scotland, 1791.
Sipe, C. Hale, *The Indian Chiefs of Pennsylvania*, Ziegler Printing Co., Butler, Pa., 1927.
———, *The Indian Wars of Pennsylvania*, The Telegraph Press, Harrisburg, 1931.
Teeple, Bruce, et. al., *In Schadde Vun Rundkopp, A Selected History of the Woodward/Fiedler Area*, Privately published compilation by area residents, 2000.
Wallace, Paul A., *Indians in Pennsylvania*, Pennsylvania Historical Commission, Harrisburg, 1970.
Waterman, Watkins & Co., *History of Bedford, Somerset, and Fulton Counties, Pa.*, Chicago, 1884.
Welfing, Mary E., *The Ole Bull Colony in Potter County One Hundredth Anniversary Observed July 31—August 1, 1952* Potter County Historical Society, Coudersport, Pa., 1952.
Welshans, Wayne O., *A Nippenose Collection*, privately published anecdotes and photos, 1995.
Wilkinson, Norman B., *Ole Bull's New Norway, Pennsylvania Leaflet #14*, Pennsylvania Historical and Museum Commission, Harrisburg, 1962.

ABOUT THE AUTHOR

JEFFREY R. FRAZIER was born and raised in Centre Hall, Centre County, where he says he grew up in a "Tom Sawyer sort of way", later graduating with a BS from Penn State in 1967, and then an MBA from Rider University in New Jersey in 1978. Some of the fondest memories of his boyhood include explorations of out-of-the-way spots in the mountains and accounts of the legends that seem to cling to them, and beginning in 1970 he began collecting those same kind of anecdotes  from all over the state; ranging from the Blue Mountains of Berks and Lehigh Counties, the South Mountains of Adams County, the "Black Forest" area of Potter and Tioga Counties, the Alleghenies of Clearfield and Blair Counties, and the other counties in the middle. He has compiled his vast collection of tales into a series titled *Pennsylvania Fireside Tales*. The *Pennsylvania Mountain Landmarks* series is a continuation of his work, written in a format that the average reader can enjoy, especially those who love the green valleys and cloud-covered mountain peaks of Pennsylvania as much as he does.

www.ingramcontent.com/pod-product-compliance
Lightning Source LLC
LaVergne TN
LVHW011423080426
835512LV00005B/240